Access Control in Data Management Systems

Synthesis Lectures on Data Management

Editor
M. Tamer Özsu, *University of Waterloo*

Synthesis Lectures on Data Management is edited by Tamer Özsu of the University of Waterloo. The series will publish 50- to 125 page publications on topics pertaining to data management. The scope will largely follow the purview of premier information and computer science conferences, such as ACM SIGMOD, VLDB, ICDE, PODS, ICDT, and ACM KDD. Potential topics include, but not are limited to: query languages, database system architectures, transaction management, data warehousing, XML and databases, data stream systems, wide scale data distribution, multimedia data management, data mining, and related subjects.

Access Control in Data Management Systems
Elena Ferrari
2010

An Introduction to Duplicate Detection
Felix Naumann and Melanie Herschel
2010

Privacy-Preserving Data Publishing: An Overview
Raymond Chi-Wing Wong and Ada Wai-Chee Fu
2010

Keyword Search in Databases
Jeffrey Xu Yu, Lu Qin, and Lijun Chang
2009

Access Control in Data Management Systems
Elena Ferrari

ISBN: 978-3-031-00708-8   paperback
ISBN: 978-3-031-01836-7   ebook

DOI 10.1007/978-3-031-01836-7

A Publication in the Springer series
SYNTHESIS LECTURES ON DATA MANAGEMENT

Lecture #4
Series Editor: M. Tamer Özsu, *University of Waterloo*
Series ISSN
Synthesis Lectures on Data Management
Print 2153-5418   Electronic 2153-5426

Access Control in Data Management Systems

Elena Ferrari
University of Insubria, Varese, Italy

SYNTHESIS LECTURES ON DATA MANAGEMENT #4

ABSTRACT

Access control is one of the fundamental services that any Data Management System should provide. Its main goal is to protect data from unauthorized read and write operations. This is particularly crucial in today's open and interconnected world, where each kind of information can be easily made available to a huge user population, and where a damage or misuse of data may have unpredictable consequences that go beyond the boundaries where data reside or have been generated.

This book provides an overview of the various developments in access control for data management systems. Discretionary, mandatory, and role-based access control will be discussed, by surveying the most relevant proposals and analyzing the benefits and drawbacks of each paradigm in view of the requirements of different application domains. Access control mechanisms provided by commercial Data Management Systems are presented and discussed. Finally, the last part of the book is devoted to discussion of some of the most challenging and innovative research trends in the area of access control, such as those related to the Web 2.0 revolution or to the Database as a Service paradigm.

This book is a valuable reference for an heterogeneous audience. It can be used as either an extended survey for people who are interested in access control or as a reference book for senior undergraduate or graduate courses in data security with a special focus on access control. It is also useful for technologists, researchers, managers, and developers who want to know more about access control and related emerging trends.

KEYWORDS

data management systems, data protection, confidentiality, integrity, access control, discretionary access control, mandatory access control, role-based access control, authorization administration

Contents

Acknowledgments xi

Preface xiii

1   Access Control: Basic Concepts 1

    1.1   Introduction 1

    1.2   Historical Prospective 1

    1.3   Data Protection 2

    1.4   Basic Components 3

    1.5   Access Control Policies 4

    1.6   Access Authorizations 6

        1.6.1   Authorization Subjects 6

        1.6.2   Authorization Objects 7

        1.6.3   Authorization Privileges 7

        1.6.4   Authorizations: Further Components 7

    1.7   Administration Policies 9

    1.8   Access Control Models 10

2   Discretionary Access Control for Relational Data Management Systems 11

    2.1   The Access Matrix Model 11

    2.2   The System R Access Control Model 13

        2.2.1   GRANT Command 14

        2.2.2   REVOKE Command 16

        2.2.3   Authorization Storage 17

        2.2.4   Authorization Management and Enforcement 18

        2.2.5   Recursive Revocation 19

        2.2.6   Authorizations on Views 22

2.3   DAC Support in SQL 25

2.4   Extensions to the System R Access Control Model 26

    2.4.1 Positive and Negative Authorizations 27

    2.4.2 Temporal Authorizations 29

2.5   Oracle Virtual Private Database 30

3   Discretionary Access Control for Advanced Data Models 37

3.1   Access Control for Object DMSs 37

3.2   Access Control for XML Data 39

    3.2.1 Access Control Requirements 40

    3.2.2 Access Control Models 41

    3.2.3 Efficiency of Access Control 46

4   Mandatory Access Control 49

4.1   Bell and LaPadula Model 50

4.2   Multilevel Relational Data Model 54

4.3   Mandatory Access Control for Object DMSs 56

4.4   MAC vs DAC 57

4.5   Information-flow Control Models 59

5   Role-based Access Control 61

5.1   The ANSI/INCITS RBAC Standard 62

    5.1.1 Core RBAC 62

    5.1.2 Hierarchical RBAC 64

    5.1.3 Constrained RBAC 65

5.2   RBAC Support in SQL 67

5.3   Role Administration 70

5.4   RBAC Extensions 74

6   Emerging Trends in Access Control 77

6.1   Access Control under the Database as a Service Model 77

6.2   Access Control for Data Stream Management Systems 80

6.3   Access Control in the Web 2.0 Era 82

    6.3.1 OSN Access Control Requirements 82

    6.3.2 Proposed Solutions 83

6.4   Further Research Directions in Access Control 85

Bibliography 89

Author's Biography 103

Acknowledgments

A work of this kind depends on the cooperation of many people, students, colleagues, and researchers who have worked with me on topics related to access control. Without their efforts this project would not have been possible. I would like to thank Barbara Carminati who read the final draft of this book and provided valuable comments. Special thanks go to M. Tamer Özsu who gave me the opportunity to write this book and provided many valuable comments to improve its quality. I really appreciate the Morgan & Claypool staff, in particular Executive Editor Diane D. Cerra for help throughout this project and Dr. C.L. Tondo and his crew for handling the production of the camera-ready pages. Last, but not least, special thanks to my family for their great and warm support through this exciting but time-consuming project. In particular, I am really indebted to my little son Tommaso Piero, to which this book is dedicated, with love.

Elena Ferrari
April 2010

Preface

We live in a time of unprecedented opportunities for storing, managing, and analyzing data referring to any kind of information, from personal to business-oriented, recorded by a variety of devices that follow us during our daily activities. This huge amount of information is both a challenge and a risk. Indeed, the availability of this source of information is the basic building block of the idea of the *knowledge society*: a society where knowledge is a major component of any human activity and decisions—big or small—can be taken on the basis of reliable knowledge, distilled from ubiquitous generated data. Moreover, the Web 2.0 revolution and its collaborative tools have made access to data easier by potentially unknown users.

In such a scenario, data become one of the most crucial assets and, as such, their protection from any kind of intrusions, improper modifications, theft, and unauthorized disclosures is a fundamental service. Therefore, there is a strong need of models and mechanisms to protect data managed by any Data Management System (DMS). Due to the open and interconnected digital world we are immersed in today, data protection is much more difficult than in the past, because it is almost impossible to design safe boundaries where data can be confined.

Data security [Ferrari, 2009c] is a broad concept that deals with different aspects of data protection (e.g., authentication, integrity, auditing). Such security properties are usually enforced through a set of *security services*, using a variety of techniques (e.g., encryption, digital signatures, trusted hardware/software).

This book is about one of the key components of the security infrastructure of any data management system, that is, *access control* [Ferrari, 2009a]. Access control aims at preventing unauthorized operations (such as read and write) on the managed data. In this book, we first examine what is needed to control access to data, then we explore the major approaches that have been applied in designing access control mechanisms. As we will see in the reminder of the book, the developments in access control are mainly driven by two factors: the development of new data models and the needs of new applications and environments. The overall goal of these developments is to provide more expressive access control models without compromising the security and efficiency of the system[1].

The book is organized as follows. We start our journey in Chapter 1 by providing the basic concepts on access control that will be developed throughout the book. Then, Chapters 2 and 3 are devoted to discretionary access control. Chapter 2 is about relational data management systems. It revises the most important research proposals as well as discusses the access control support provided by SQL and some of the most innovative features provided by relational DMSs. Chapter 3 is devoted to discretionary access control, however it considers data models beyond the relational one and, in

---

[1] Here, and in what follows, expressivity is related to the set of access control requirements that the access control model possibly supports.

particular, the object and XML data models. We believe that the discussion of access control for XML data is fundamental due to the role played by XML for Web data management. Chapter 4 is devoted to the other big family of access control models, besides discretionary ones, that is, mandatory access control models. Besides describing the most relevant proposals in the field, we discuss the main differences with respect to discretionary access control, the environments that can benefit from mandatory access control, as well as the possible drawbacks that have to be considered. Chapter 5 is devoted to the third major player in the access control area, that is, Role-based Access Control (RBAC). We describe the ANSI/INCITS RBAC standard and some of its recent developments. One of the primary goals of RBAC is to simplify administration of access rights. Therefore, a part of the chapter is devoted to discussing the administration models for RBAC proposed so far. In Chapter 6, we highlight several interesting research issues regarding access control; for instance, how to protect data when they are outsourced to a third party, how to protect data streams that should be securely managed on-the-fly, and how to protect resources and personal information in an On-line Social Network. All these environments pose new and fascinating challenges for what concerns access control that sometimes requires rethinking the way access control has been managed so far.

An heterogeneous audience can benefit from this book. First of all, the book could be used as a reference for senior undergraduate or graduate courses in data security which has a special focus on access control. However, it is also useful for technologists, researchers, managers, and developers who want to know more about access control and emerging trends.

Elena Ferrari
April 2010

CHAPTER 1

Access Control: Basic Concepts

1.1 INTRODUCTION

Access control [Bertino and Sandhu, 2005; Ferrari, 2009a; Ferrari and Thuraisingham, 2000] is one of the most relevant services provided by any Data Management System (DMS). Its overall goal is to protect the managed data from unauthorized operations. In this chapter, we provide the basic concepts on access control and data protection needed to understand the various access control models and mechanisms discussed in the rest of the book. We start with a brief history of the main developments in the field of access control. Then, we cast access control in the more general field of data protection. In the subsequent sections, we illustrate the basic components of access control, that is, access control policies and authorizations. Authorization management is described in Section 1.7 and Section 1.8 ends with a brief introduction of the main access control paradigms.

1.2 HISTORICAL PROSPECTIVE

A DMS exploits the services of the underlying operating system to manage its data (for instance, to store data into files), and this also applies to access control. This is one of the reasons why access control models for DMSs have been greatly influenced by the models developed for the protection of Operating System (OS) resources, such as the model proposed by Lampson [1971], known also as the *access matrix model* (see Section 2.1 for a description of this model).

Much of the early work on data protection was on inference control in statistical databases. Then, in the 1970s, as research in relational databases began, attention was directed toward access control. A lot of early work on access control for relational database systems [Fagin, 1976; Griffiths and Wade, 1976] was done as part of the research on System R at IBM Almaden Research Center. The developed model strongly influenced most of the subsequent research activities as well as the access control models and mechanisms of current commercial relational DMSs (see Section 2.2 for more details on this topic). At the same time, some early work on mandatory access control for Data Management Systems began, but it was the Airforce Summer Study [Air Force Studies Board, 1983] that started much of the developments in this field. Later, in the mid-1980s, pioneering research was carried out at SRI International and Honeywell Inc. on systems such as SeaView and LOCK Data View [Castano et al., 1995]. Some of the technologies developed by these research efforts were transferred to commercial products by corporations such as Oracle, Sybase, and Informix. In the 1990s, numerous other developments started, mainly to meet the access control requirements of new applications and environments, such as the World Wide Web, data warehouses and decision support systems, distributed, active, and multimedia DMSs, workflow management systems, collaborative systems, and, more recently, peer-to-peer systems, geographical information systems, and data stream management systems. This has resulted in several extensions to the basic access control models previously developed, by including, for instance, the support for temporal constraints, derivation rules, positive and negative authorizations, strong and weak authorizations, and content and context-dependent authorizations. Some of these developments have also been partially transferred to commercial DMSs (for instance, see Oracle Virtual Private Database described in Section 2.5). In the mid-1990s, Role-based Access Control (RBAC) was proposed [Sandhu et al., 1996] as a way to simplify authorization management within companies and organizations. In the 2000s, there have been numerous other developments in the field of access control, mainly driven by developments in Web data management. For example, standards such as XML (eXtensible Markup Language), RDF (Resource Description Framework), and all the technologies related to the Semantic Web require proper access control mechanisms [Carminati et al., 2006]. Also, Web Services are becoming extremely popular and therefore research is currently carried on to address the related access control issues [Ferrari and Thuraisingham, 2004]. Access control is also currently being examined for new application areas such as Database as a Service [Ferrari, 2009b] and location-based services [Decker, 2008]. Additionally, privacy is becoming a primary concern and this has been reflected in research work trying to enhance protection mechanisms for DMSs with the protection of personal data [Agrawal et al., 2005; Byun and Li, 2008; Ni et al., 2009].

Other interesting developments are related to the Web 2.0 revolution that has evolved the Web from a simple tool for publishing textual data into a complex collaborative knowledge management system. This evolution is mainly due to the rapid spread of social computing services, such as blogs, wikis, social networks, and social bookmarking services. The management of this huge and complex knowledge base poses several new challenges and requires complete re-design of the way we assure protection to the managed data. Some of these new trends will be discussed in Chapter 6.

1.3   DATA PROTECTION

Traditionally, protecting data stored into a DMS requires addressing three main issues:

- **Data secrecy** or **confidentiality**, that is, preventing improper or unauthorized read operations on the managed data. When data are related to personal information, the term *privacy* is used. However, it is important to note that protecting privacy requires some additional countermeasures with respect to those employed to ensure data confidentiality. For instance, additional factors must be taken into account, such as the data retention period, the user consent, or the purpose for which data are collected (see Bonchi and Ferrari [2010]; Li [2005] for more details on privacy-preserving data management systems).

- **Data integrity**, that is, protecting data from unauthorized or improper modifications or deletions.

- **Data availability**, that is, prevention and recovery from hardware and software errors and from malicious data denial attacks making the data or some of their portions unavailable to authorized users.

Generally, each of the above security properties is ensured by more than one DMS service. The *access control mechanism*, which is the focus of this book, is one of the most relevant security services, since it is the basis of enforcing both data confidentiality and integrity.

Indeed, whenever a user tries to access a data object, the access control mechanism checks the rights of the subject against the set of specified *authorizations*. The access is granted only if it does not conflict with the stated authorizations. Data confidentiality is also obtained through the use of *encryption techniques* [Stallings, 2003], either applied to the data stored on secondary storage or when data are transmitted on the network, to prevent an intruder from intercepting the data and access their contents. Besides the access control mechanism, data integrity is also ensured by *integrity constraints*, provided by most of current DMSs. Integrity constraints allow one to express correctness conditions on the stored data, and therefore avoid incorrect data updates and deletions. These constraints are automatically checked by the DMS upon the request for each update operation. Furthermore, digital signature techniques are applied to detect improper data modifications. They are also used to ensure data authenticity. Finally, the recovery subsystem and the concurrency control mechanism ensure that data are available and correct despite hardware and software failures and despite data accesses from concurrent application programs. Data availability, especially for data that are available on the Web, can be further enhanced by the use of techniques avoiding query floods [Squicciarini et al., 2008] or other Denial-of-Service (DoS) attacks.

In this book, we focus on access control mechanisms and related access control models. We refer the reader to any database textbook (e.g., Garcia-Molina et al. [2008]) for an extensive discussion of recovery and concurrency control mechanisms, and for details on integrity constraints.

It is important to note that an access control mechanism basically regulates data accesses of users which have been already authorized to use the services of the DMS. Therefore, for its proper functioning it must rely on some authentication mechanism which identifies users and confirms their identities [Blanton, 2009].

1.4   BASIC COMPONENTS

Access control is usually performed against a set of *authorizations* stated by Security Administrators (SAs) or users according to the *access control policies* of the organization. An access control policy defines the high-level rules according to which access control must be regulated. These may depend on many heterogeneous factors, such as the in-force legislation, the domain in which the owner of the data operates (e.g., business, education, healthcare), local rules, or the specific user requirements. Simple examples of access control policies are: "*Psychological evaluations of employees can be seen only by their managers*" or "*Drugs prescribed to a patient while he/she is in the hospital can be seen only by his/her family doctor once the patient has been discharged*".

Access control policies can be seen as high-level requirements concerning data protection that, in order to be automatically enforced, should be translated into a set of authorizations. An authorization states which subjects can perform which actions on which objects and, optionally, under which condition. Authorizations are stored into the DMS and are then used to verify whether or not an access request can be authorized. How to represent and store authorizations depends on the protected resources, but the standard way is to use a uniform representation for authorizations and the managed data. For instance, in a relational DMS, authorizations are usually modeled as tuples stored into system catalogs. In contrast, when resources to be protected are XML data, authorizations are usually encoded using XML itself.

Example 1.1   Consider once again the access control policy: "*Psychological evaluations of employees can be seen only by their managers*" and suppose there are three employees Ann, Bob, and Chris. Suppose, moreover, that Ann is the manager of Bob. Let $PEval_B$ be a file containing the psychological evaluation of Bob. Authorization (Ann,$PEval_B$,read) correctly enforces the policy since Ann is the manager of Bob, whereas the authorization (Chris,$PEval_B$,read) is not entailed by the policy since Chris is not Bob's manager.

Authorizations are expressed according to an *access control model*, which provides a formal representation of the authorizations and their enforcement. The formalization allows the proof of a set of properties (e.g., security, complexity) on the corresponding access control systems.

Authorizations are then processed by the *access control mechanism* (or *reference monitor*) to decide whether each access request can be authorized (totally or partially) or should be denied. The reference monitor is a trusted software module in charge of enforcing access control. It intercepts each access request submitted to the system (for instance, SQL statements in case of relational DMSs) and, on the basis of the specified authorizations, it determines whether the access can be partially or totally authorized, or it should be denied. The reference monitor should be *non-bypassable*, that is, it should mediate each access request. Additionally, the hardware and software architecture should ensure that the reference monitor is *tamper proof*, that is, it cannot be maliciously modified (or at least that any improper modification can be detected). Main components of access control and their interactions are illustrated in Figure 1.1.

1.5   ACCESS CONTROL POLICIES

As we have seen in the previous section, access control policies are high-level guidelines according to which accesses are regulated in the system. Therefore, they have to deal with several different dimensions. One key dimension is how much information a user should be allowed to access. In this respect, we have two main general principles.

- **Need to know (Principle of least privilege)**. This is a very conservative principle according to which each user must be able to access only those information that are necessary to his/her legitimate purpose.

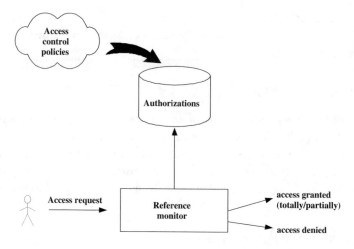

Figure 1.1: Access control: main components.

- **Maximized sharing**. This principle allows the maximum sharing of information among the users, still preserving the confidentiality/integrity of some highly sensitive information.

Both principles have some advantages and drawbacks. The main advantage of need to know is its strong protection guarantees; the drawback is that it may result in an overprotected system where some accesses that would not violate the security of the system are nevertheless prevented. Moreover, this principle may be very difficult to fully implement because it is hard to precisely determine the least amount of privileges each user needs. In contrast, the maximized sharing principle has the advantage of allowing the satisfaction of the maximum number of access requests, however its full applicability is limited to environments where information protection is not a primary concern.

A further distinction is between *open* and *closed* systems. In a closed system, nothing is allowed *except* what is explicitly granted by an authorization. According to this principle, which is the one adopted by most commercial DMSs, an authorization states the privileges granted to a user. Therefore, a closed system can be used to implement the need to know principle in that each user may receive the authorizations corresponding to the least amount of privileges he/she needs. In contrast, an open system is a system where by default access to all the resources is granted *unless* an explicit denial has been specified. Therefore, in an open system authorizations are *negative* in that they are used to specify prohibitions. An open system can easily implement the principle of maximized sharing by specifying a negative authorization only for each sensitive resource that must be kept reserved. All the other resources are by default accessible. Clearly, a closed system offers stronger security guarantees with respect to an open one. For instance, the accidental deletion of an authorization does not make the system less secure since it restricts the set of accesses that can be performed; in contrast, in an open system, since authorizations are used to express denials, the accidental removal of an authorization will result in the grant of a non-authorized privilege. This is one of the reasons why most access control mechanisms provided by commercial DMSs are based on the closed system assumption.

1.6   ACCESS AUTHORIZATIONS

The basic building block on which access control relies is a set of *authorizations*, which state who can access which resource and under which mode. In its basic form, an authorization can be conceptually modeled as a triple *(s,o,p)* that specifies that *subject s* is authorized to exercise *privilege p* on *object o*. This basic format can be extended to take into account further information in the access control process (see Section 1.6.4). However, in what follows, we start to describe the meaning of these three basic components.

1.6.1   AUTHORIZATION SUBJECTS

Authorization subjects are the "active" entities in the system, that is, those that require access to the protected data. They are therefore an abstraction of any active entity that performs computation in the system. Subjects can be classified into the following categories:

- **users**, that is, individuals logging into the system;

- **groups**, that is, sets of users;

- **roles**, that is, specific job functions within an organization with an associated collection of privileges needed to perform the activities connected to the corresponding job functions (see Chapter 5 for more details);

- **processes**, executing programs on behalf of users.

As will be described in the following chapters, the above subject categories are not mutually exclusive. For instance, some access control models may support all the categories of subjects described above, others only some of them (e.g., users and groups).

Roles and groups may be hierarchically organized. Hierarchical organization of subjects is usually a means of reducing the burden of authorization administration in that the hierarchy usually entails a *propagation principle* according to which authorization propagates along the hierarchy. The semantics of the hierarchy and the way authorizations propagate along it depend on the kind of subject being considered. For instance, the hierarchy imposed on groups usually reflects the membership of a group in another group. Therefore, authorizations propagate down the hierarchy, in that an authorization given to a group is equivalent to giving the same authorization to all the group members. In contrast, the role hierarchy usually reflects the relative position of roles within an organization. The higher the level of a role in the hierarchy, the higher its position in the organization. Therefore, authorizations usually propagate up the hierarchy.

1.6.2   AUTHORIZATION OBJECTS

Authorization objects are the "passive" components of an access control system, in that they are an abstraction of the resources to which protection from unauthorized accesses should be given. The set of objects to be protected depends on the considered environment. Files and directories are examples of objects of an operating system environment, relations, views, tuples, and attributes are examples of resources for a relational DMS, whereas user profiles are examples of resources to be protected in a social network. On the basis of the adopted access control model, authorizations can be specified at different *granularity levels*, that is, on a whole object or only on some of its components. Fine-grained access control is a useful feature when an object (e.g., a relation) contains information (e.g., tuples) of different sensitivity levels and that therefore require a differentiated protection. As in the case of subjects, objects can also be hierarchically organized. The semantics of the object hierarchy depends on the underlying data model (e.g., object-oriented, XML) but it usually represents a "part-of" relation, that is, how objects are organized in terms of other objects. Similar to subject hierarchies, the object hierarchy entails a notion of authorization propagation in that an authorization given on an object usually implies an authorization on each of its components.

1.6.3   AUTHORIZATION PRIVILEGES

Authorization privileges (or access modes) state the types of operations that a subject can exercise on the objects in the system. As with objects, the set of privileges depends on the resources to be protected. For instance, read, write, and execute privileges are typical of an operating system environment, whereas in a relational DMS privileges refer to operations that can be requested through SQL commands (e.g., select, insert, update, delete). Moreover, other less traditional environments, such as digital libraries, are characterized by new access modes, such as the usage or copying access rights, whereas in a social network environment we may have the post privilege to post a message on a user wall. An hierarchical organization of privileges is possible, which usually represents a subsumption relation among privileges. Privileges toward the bottom of the hierarchy are subsumed by privileges toward the top (for instance, the write privilege can be at a higher level in the hierarchy with respect to the read privilege, since write usually subsumes read operations). Even in this case, the rationale behind the hierarchical organization of privileges is to limit the number of authorizations to be specified in that an authorization for a privilege implies an analogous authorization for all the privileges it subsumes.

The notion of derived authorizations has been further extended in the context of logic-based access control models (e.g., Bertino et al. [2000b, 2003]; Bonatti and Olmedilla [2007]; Jajodia et al. [2001]) to support arbitrary derivation rules, not necessarily based on the hierarchical organization of objects, subjects, and privileges.

1.6.4   AUTHORIZATIONS: FURTHER COMPONENTS

In the previous sections we have seen that the basic components of an access authorization are subjects, objects and privileges. However, it may often be the case that further information should be taken into account to determine an access control decision. Therefore, a lot of research has been done with the aim of extending the basic authorization format [Ferrari and Thuraisingham, 2000]. All these extensions are driven by the goal of augmenting the expressive power of the authorization language in terms of access control requirements it may express. A first direction in this respect is to enhance the way objects and subjects are denoted in an authorization.

- *Subject specification*. It is often useful to specify authorizations based on subject characteristics, rather than on their identity (for example, a user can be given access to an R rated video, only if he/she is older than 18 years, or a user can be given access to a movie only if he/she has paid a particular type of subscription). Subject attributes are usually encoded into a *profile* or *credential*, that may be partially or totally certified by a trusted party. Besides those stored into credentials/profiles, other subject properties may be relevant for access control. For instance, in a social network, access control is mainly *relationship-based* [Carminati and Ferrari, 2008], that is, access to a resource is granted provided that between the requestor and the resource owner there exists a direct or indirect relation of a specific type. In access control models where access decisions are not only based on subject identity, the subject component of an authorization is extended with the possibility of containing a predicate (or a boolean combination of predicates) expressing conditions on the subject properties.

- *Object specification*. Besides providing access at different granularity levels, authorized objects may also be identified on the basis of conditions on their content (usually this is referred to as *content-dependent* access control). As an example, in a relational DMS supporting content-dependent access control, it is possible to authorize a subject to access information only of those employees whose salary is not greater than 50K. There are two most common approaches according to which content-based access control is enforced. The first approach is to define a view which selects the objects whose content satisfies a given condition, and then granting the authorization on the view instead of on the basic objects. This solution has been exploited in the context of relational DMSs and, more recently for XML data (cfr. Section 3.2) and data streams (cfr. Section 6.2). The second solution is to extend the object specification with the possibility of specifying a predicate (or a boolean combination of predicates) on the object content (for instance, all the documents dealing with cooking). Clearly, the enforcement of such authorizations is conditioned to the availability of a set of metadata describing the object content (e.g., keywords, tags).

Other extensions are related to the temporal dimension that is common in authorizations and it is not captured by the basic format (see, e.g., Bertino et al. [1998a, 2000a, 2001a]; Joshi et al. [2005]). These extensions are motivated by the fact that, in many situations, an authorization should hold only for a specific time period (for instance, because of resource optimization or to obtain stronger security guarantees). Moreover, there must be some temporal relations between the authorizations given to different subjects. For instance, a user may be given access to a document each time another user has the same authorization. This paradigm has been generalized to the notion of *context-based* authorizations [McDaniel, 2003], which is supported by access control models where the access control decision depends on the context in which the request has been issued (e.g., time, location, IP address).

1.7 ADMINISTRATION POLICIES

Access control administration deals with granting and revoking of authorizations. This function is usually regulated by proper *administration policies* that state who can grant and revoke privileges to other subjects, or perform other administrative operations related to access control, such as creation and deletion of roles. Administration policies may be classified according to the following categories [Ferrari, 2009d]:

- **SA administration**. According to this policy, only the Security Administrator(s) can perform administrative operations regarding access control. Main advantages of this policy are in terms of simplicity of the implementation and on the strict control performed over the managed data in that only one trusted entity (or few) is in charge of authorization management. The main disadvantage is that it is highly centralized (even though different SAs can manage authorization administration for different portions of the data) and therefore it is seldom used in practice, apart from very simple systems.

- **Owner administration**. This is the policy commonly adopted by DMSs and OSs. According to this policy, the creator of an object becomes its owner and he/she is the only one authorized to grant and revoke authorizations on the object.

- **Joint administration**. Under this policy, particularly suited for collaborative environments, several subjects are jointly responsible for administering specific authorizations. For instance, under the joint administration policy it can be required that the authorization to write a certain document is given by two different users, for instance with two different functions within an organization. Authorizations for a subject to access an object require that all the administrators (or the majority of them) of the object issue a grant request.

Administration policies can be further combined with *administration delegation*, according to which the administrator of an object can grant other subjects the right to grant and revoke authorizations on the object. Delegation can also be specified for selected privileges, for example only for read operations. Most current DMSs support the owner administration policy with delegation (see Chapter 2 for more details).

Finally, note that the joint administration policy is becoming more and more important in the Web 2.0 scenario, where social computing services require going beyond the owner administration policy. For instance, if we consider the social network scenario, it is clear that this collaborative environment requires taking into account additional subjects-to-objects relationships, besides the traditional ownership one. For example, if we consider a general purpose social network like Facebook, users "own" a photo, but they can also be "tagged" to a photo; they can "post" a comment to a wall, but also they can "reply " to an existing post. In this context, a joint administration policy seems more appropriate, requiring, for instance, the consent of the tagged users before the release of a photo.

1.8   ACCESS CONTROL MODELS

A basic distinction when dealing with access control is between *discretionary* and *mandatory* access control. Discretionary Access Control (DAC) governs the access of subjects to objects on the basis of subjects' identity and a set of authorizations that state, for each subject, the set of objects that he/she can access in the system and the allowed access modes. When an access request is submitted to the system, the access control mechanism verifies whether the access can be authorized or not according to the specified authorizations. The system is discretionary in the sense that a subject, by proper configuration of the set of authorizations, is able both to enforce various access control requirements, and to dynamically change them when needed (simply by updating the authorization state). In contrast, in Mandatory Access Control (MAC) the accesses that subjects can exercise on the objects in the system are derived from subjects and objects security classification [Ferrari and Thuraisingham, 2000]. The security classification of an object is a measure of the sensitivity of the information it conveys (the higher is the classification, the higher is the protection that must be assured). In contrast, the subject classification is a measure of how much the subject is trustworthy with respect to information released to unauthorized subjects. This type of security has also been referred to as *multilevel security*, and DMSs that enforce multilevel access control are called *Multilevel Secure Data Management Systems* (MLS/DMSs). When mandatory access control is enforced, authorizations are implicitly derived by subjects and objects security classes. Indeed, the decision as to whether to grant an access or not depends on the access mode and the relation existing between the classification of the subject requesting the access and that of the requested object. MAC and DAC policies are not mutually exclusive. If they are jointly applied, then an access is granted only of it is allowed by both MAC and DAC. In addition to DAC and MAC, *Role-Based Access Control* (RBAC) has been more recently proposed [Sandhu et al., 1996]. RBAC is an alternative to DAC and MAC, mainly conceived for regulating accesses within companies and organizations. In RBAC, permissions are associated with roles, instead of with users, and users acquire permissions through their membership to roles. The set of authorizations can be inferred by the sets of user-role and role-permission assignments. DAC is covered by Chapters 2 and 3, whereas MAC and RBAC are described in Chapters 4 and 5, respectively.

CHAPTER 2

Discretionary Access Control for Relational Data Management Systems

Most of the access control mechanisms of current data management systems enforce discretionary access control (DAC) (see Section 1.8). The main reason is the flexibility of DAC, in terms of protection requirements it can support, that makes it suitable for a variety of contexts in the commercial as well as in the industrial environments.

This chapter is devoted to explaining how discretionary access control is enforced in relational DMSs. We start by briefly describing the access matrix model, which, although it has been mainly developed for the protection of operating systems, has highly inspired most of the discretionary models later developed for data management systems. Then, in Section 2.2 we describe the System R access control model [Griffiths and Wade, 1976], a milestone in the field of access control that has inspired most of the research in access control, as well as the access control mechanisms provided by commercial relational DMSs. In Section 2.3, we briefly review the support for discretionary access control provided by the SQL standard. Section 2.4 presents some of the main extensions proposed to the System R access control model, whereas Section 2.5 presents the innovative DAC features provided by Oracle Virtual Private Database.

2.1 THE ACCESS MATRIX MODEL

Among the models developed for operating systems the one that has most influenced access control models for DMSs is the model defined by Lampson [1971], later refined by Graham and Denning [1972] and formalized by Harrison et al. [1975] (*HRU model*). This model is the conceptual reference model to represent authorizations in system adopting DAC. In what follows, we present only the basic concepts of this model, whereas we refer the interested readers to Graham and Denning [1972]; Harrison et al. [1975]; Lampson [1971] for all the details.

The name of the model derives from how the authorization state is represented within the system, that is, as a matrix. More precisely, in the access matrix model, the authorizations currently holding in the system are represented as a triple (S, O, M), where: S is the set of authorization subjects, O is the set of objects to be protected, and M is the *access matrix*. In the access matrix, rows denote subjects, columns denote objects, and the element $M[i, j]$ contains the privileges that

	marc.doc	edit.exe	games.dir
Marc	read,write	execute	execute
Ann	–	execute	execute,read,write

Figure 2.1:   An example of access matrix.

subject s_i holds on object o_j. An access is granted only if there is the corresponding privilege in the access matrix.

Example 2.1   Figure 2.1 shows an example of access matrix. For instance, with reference to Figure 2.1, both Marc and Ann can run the programs stored in directory games.dir. In contrast, only Ann can modify and read the files contained in this directory, whereas Marc is the only user authorized to read and modify the file marc.doc.

Although the matrix represents a good and intuitive conceptual representation of authorizations, it is not appropriate for real implementations since, usually, the access matrix will be enormous in size and will be sparse (most of its cells are likely to be empty). This is because, typically, subjects have access only to limited portions of the data managed by a data management system. Storing the matrix as a two-dimensional array is therefore a waste of memory space. Thus, there are two main alternative approaches to implementing the access matrix in real systems:

- **Access Control List (ACL)**. The access matrix is implemented through a set of lists, one for each object (i.e., the columns of the matrix) in the system. The list associated with an object has an element for each subject holding a privilege on the object. This element contains the set of privileges the subject can exercise on the object. This is the way usually adopted by modern operating systems.

- **Capability List**. The access matrix is implemented through a set of lists associated with the subjects (i.e., the rows in the matrix) in the system. The capability list of a subject contains an element for each object which can be accessed by the subject. The element contains the list of privileges the subjects can exercise on the object. This approach can be suitable to distributed systems, where subjects can request access to objects hosted by different nodes. For instance, a user can authenticate once, gains his/her capabilities, and then uses them at the various hosts composing the system to get access to the protected objects. However, the system should be equipped with mechanisms avoiding the use of fake or invalid capabilities (e.g., those referring to revoked privileges).

As we mentioned at the beginning of this chapter, the access matrix model and, more generally, the access models developed for OSs, have greatly influenced the models developed for the protection of DMSs, such as the System R access control model presented in the next section.

However, also it should be noticed that protecting the two environments has many substantial differences, that require the development of ad-hoc mechanisms for DMSs. In particular, protecting data stored in a DMS requires addressing further issues besides those faced in an OS environment. One of the main reasons for this is that the data model of a DMS is usually richer than that of an OS. For instance, in a relational DMS data are represented at different levels of abstraction (i.e., physical, logical, view level), whereas an operating system adopts a unique representation of data (that is, data are stored in files) and this simplifies their protection. Furthermore, in a DMS different abstractions are used to represent data at the logical level (e.g., relations, objects/classes, XML files) that require different ways of protections. Furthermore, DMSs usually require a variety of granularity levels for access control. For instance, in a relational DMS data can be protected at the relation or view level. However, sometimes finer granularity levels are needed, such as selected attributes or selected tuples within a table, since different attributes/tuples may have different sensitivity. The same applies if we use XML to represent data. Sometimes, a whole document (or all the documents conforming to an XMLSchema) has the same protection requirements; sometimes, different elements within the same document must be protected differently. Other times, we need a finer granularity in that selected attributes within an element need differentiated protection (e.g., attribute salary within an employee element). In contrast, in an operating system data protection is usually enforced at the file level. Another difference between the two environments is that in a DMS, objects at the logical level are usually related by different semantic relations, and these relations must be carefully protected (for instance, in a relational DMS, data in different tables are linked through foreign keys). Moreover, several logical objects (e.g., different views) may correspond to the same physical object (e.g., the same file), or the same logical object (e.g., a view) may correspond to different physical/logical objects (e.g., different files/relations on which the view has been built). These issues do not have to be considered when protecting data in an operating system. Finally, data in a database are usually accessed through a variety of access modes (e.g., in a relational DMS access modes roughly correspond to those that can be exercised through SQL statements), whereas in an OS access modes are usually read, write, and execute.

In the following section, we will see how some of these issues have been addressed by the System R access control model.

2.2 THE SYSTEM R ACCESS CONTROL MODEL

A milestone in the history of access control is the discretionary access control model proposed by Griffiths and Wade [1976], and later revised by Fagin [1976], in the framework of the relational DMS System R, a prototype system developed at the IBM Research Laboratory at San Jose. The importance of System R access control model relies on the fact that this model has influenced most of the research subsequently done on DAC, and it has also served as a basis for the development of most of the authorization mechanisms provided as part of commercial DMSs, such as those provided by Oracle or DB2, as well as for the SQL standard [ISO, 2003].

Since the model has been designed for the protection of relational databases, objects to be protected are either relations or views. For simplicity, in what follows, we use the term "relation" to refer to both views and base relations, unless a distinction between the two is needed.

Privileges supported by the model correspond to those executable through an SQL command (e.g., `select`, `insert`, `delete`, `update`). Subjects are users requiring access to relations through the issuing of SQL commands. Groups and roles are not supported in the original formulation of the model.

Authorization administration is ownership-based with delegation (cfr. Section 1.7). Therefore, whenever a user creates a relation, he/she receives all the supported privileges defined on it. Additionally, he/she can grant or revoke other users all the privileges (except drop) on the created relation. Moreover, the owner of a relation can grant authorizations with the *grant option*. If a user owns an authorization for a privilege on a relation with the grant option, he/she can grant the privilege, as well as the grant option, to other users.

In what follows, we first illustrate the main commands to modify the authorization state (that is, `GRANT` and `REVOKE`). Then, we discuss how authorizations are stored and managed, and how access control is enforced. In Section 2.2.5, we deal with the semantics of the revoke operation, which should be carefully considered due to administration delegation. Finally, in Section 2.2.6 we show how authorizations on views are used in the System R access control model to both increase the flexibility of the model in terms of requirements it may support and to provide better security guarantees.

2.2.1   GRANT COMMAND

Authorizations are specified through the `GRANT` command, with the following SQL-like syntax[1]:

```
GRANT {<privileges> | ALL[PRIVILEGES]}
ON <relation>
TO {<users> | PUBLIC} [WITH GRANT OPTION];
```

where:

- `<privileges>` is the set of privileges granted through the command. Therefore, a single grant command can be used to grant more than one privilege (the privileges should be separated by a comma in the `GRANT` command). Keywords `ALL` and `ALL PRIVILEGES` are a shortcut to denote all the supported privileges.

- `<relation>` is the name of the relation on which the privileges are granted.

- `<users>` denotes the set of users to which the grant command applies. If the keyword `PUBLIC` is used, authorizations granted through the command apply to all the users in the system.

---

[1] Here and in what follows, to present the SQL syntax we use square brackets to denote optional parts of a command, and curly brackets to denote alternative components, divided by symbol '|', from which one should be mandatory selected. Moreover, we use capital letters to denote SQL reserved keywords, even if the language is case insensitive apart from values of string type.

- The optional clause WITH GRANT OPTION allows the grantor to delegate privilege administration. If the grant option is not specified, than the users receiving the privileges have only the right to exercise them, but not giving them to others. In contrast, when the grant option is specified, the users receiving the privileges can also grant the received privileges to other users.

All the privileges that can be specified in a GRANT command apply to whole relations. The only exception is the update privilege for which the set of attributes to which it applies can be specified, with the format update($a_1, \ldots, a_n$), where $a_1, \ldots, a_n$ are selected attributes within the relation in the GRANT command.

Example 2.2   As a running example throughout the book, we consider a database that stores information about the customers and videos offered by a video library. In particular, customer information (e.g., name, address, phone number) are stored into the relation Customers, whereas information about the videos and the corresponding movies are stored into relations Videos and Movies, respectively. Suppose that Leo is the owner of relations Videos, Customers, and Movies. The following are examples of GRANT commands[2]:

```
Leo: GRANT update(phone) ON Customers TO Marc;
Leo: GRANT select ON Videos TO Beth, Gena WITH GRANT OPTION;
Gena: GRANT select ON Videos TO Matt;
Leo: GRANT ALL PRIVILEGES ON Movies, Videos TO Helen WITH GRANT OPTION;
Helen: GRANT insert, select ON Videos TO Beth;
```

With the first command Leo authorizes Marc to update the attribute phone of the tuples stored in relation Customers, whereas by the second command he grants Gena and Beth the privilege to query the Videos relation. Since the privilege is granted with the grant option, Beth and Gena can also authorize other users to query the Videos relation. Therefore, they become administrators of the Videos relation with respect to the select privilege. Because of this, Gena grants Matt the select privilege on Videos through the third command. The fourth command authorizes Helen to exercise all the supported privileges on the relations Movies and Videos. These privileges are granted with the grant option and therefore Helen becomes a further administrator of the two relations. Due to this privilege, Helen specifies the fifth command, by which she authorizes Beth to insert and select tuples from the Videos relation.

Since the System R access control model supports administration delegation, it may happen that a user receives the same privilege on the same relation twice or more (from different users). For instance, with reference to Example 2.2, Bett receives twice the privilege to select tuples from the

---

[2]We use notation u: to specify that user u is the *grantor* of the authorizations, that is, the user who requests the execution of the GRANT command.

`Videos` relation, one from Leo (with grant option) and the other from Helen (without the grant option). As we will see in Section 2.2.5, this impacts the side effects of privilege revocation.

Moreover, the privileges a user holds may be divided into two groups: those that have been received with the grant option, that is, the *grantable privileges*, and those that have been received without the grant option, that is, the *non-grantable privileges*. For access control enforcement, both these two sets of privileges must be checked, whereas to decide the result of a `GRANT` command only the grantable privileges should be considered (see Section 2.2.4 for more details).

2.2.2   REVOKE COMMAND

The `REVOKE` command is used to revoke privileges previously granted through a `GRANT` command. Its syntax is as follows:

```
REVOKE {<privileges> | ALL[PRIVILEGES]}
ON <relation>
FROM {<users> | PUBLIC};
```

where:

- `<privileges>` denotes the set of privileges to be revoked. Keywords `ALL` or `ALL PRIVILEGES` denote that all the previously granted privileges are revoked to the users listed in the `REVOKE` command.

- `<relation>` denotes the name of the relation on which the privileges are revoked.

- `<users>` is the set of users to which the privileges are revoked. Keyword `PUBLIC` is a shortcut for all the users to which the privileges have been previously granted.

Each user can only issue `REVOKE` commands referring to privileges he/she previously granted. A `REVOKE` command implies the revocation also of the grant option.

Example 2.3   Let us consider the `GRANT` commands of Example 2.2 and the following `REVOKE` commands, issued by Leo:

```
REVOKE update, insert ON Movies FROM Helen;
REVOKE update ON Customers FROM Marc;
REVOKE select ON Videos FROM Gena;
```

The first command revokes Helen the authorization to insert and modify tuples in the `Movies` relation. It also revokes the privilege to authorize other users to perform such operations. The second command revokes Marc the right to update the `phone` attribute of the tuples stored into the `Customers` relation. Finally, the third command revokes Gena the right to query relation `Videos`.

Since a user may receive the same authorization from different sources, the execution of a REVOKE command does not always imply that the involved user loses the revoked privileges, as the following example shows.

Example 2.4   Let us consider the GRANT commands of Example 2.2 and the following REVOKE command:

    Leo: REVOKE select ON Videos FROM Beth, Gena;

After the execution of this command, Gena is no longer allowed to query the Videos relation, whereas Beth can still query the relation due to the authorization she received from Helen. What she looses is the possibility of granting other users the select privilege on Videos.

2.2.3   AUTHORIZATION STORAGE

System R uses a uniform representation for authorizations and data. Therefore, authorizations are stored into two system catalogs, called Sysauth and Syscolauth, respectively. Sysauth stores information on the privileges granted on the objects in the system, whereas Syscolauth is used to manage the update privilege that, different from the other ones, can apply on selected attributes within a relation. More precisely, Sysauth schema consists of the following attributes:

- user: the id of the user to which privileges are granted;

- rel: the name of the relation on which privileges are granted;

- type $\in$ {R,V} denotes whether the privileges are granted on a relation (type='R') or on a view (type='V');

- select: it denotes whether the user has the privilege to query the specified relation. The value of this attribute is a *timestamp*, representing the time at which the privilege has been granted. If the value is 0, this means that the user does not hold the privilege. Sysauth contains an attribute with a similar semantics for each distinct access mode supported by the model;

- grantor: the id of the user who granted the privileges;

- grantopt $\in$ {Y,N}, specifies whether the privileges are grantable (grantopt ='Y') or not (grantopt ='N').

Timestamp information are needed to correctly manage revoke operations (See Section 2.2.5). The timestamp can be the value of a counter or it can denote a real time instant. The only requirement is that it satisfies the following two properties: *(i)* it monotonically increases; *(ii)* no two GRANT

user	rel	type	select	insert	update	grantor	grantopt
Leo	Customers	R	20	20	20		Y
Leo	Videos	R	22	22	22		Y
Leo	Movies	R	25	25	25		Y
Marc	Customers	R	0	0	30	Leo	N
Beth	Videos	R	32	0	0	Leo	Y
Gena	Videos	R	32	0	0	Leo	Y
Matt	Videos	R	35	0	0	Gena	N
Helen	Videos	R	40	40	40	Leo	Y
Helen	Movies	R	40	40	40	Leo	Y
Beth	Videos	R	47	47	0	Helen	N

Figure 2.2: An example of Sysauth catalog.

commands exist with the same timestamp. Privileges granted through the same GRANT command have the same timestamp.

Example 2.5   Figure 2.2 reports an example of entries in Sysauth referring to the select, insert, and update privileges and relations Customers, Videos, and Movies. The portion of Sysauth in Figure 2.2 refers to the authorization state after the execution of the GRANT commands in Example 2.2. Timestamps have been arbitrarily assigned based on the constraints described above. Note that the first three tuples in the catalog have been automatically inserted when the three relations have been created by Leo. The timestamp denotes the time of the CREATE TABLE command.

Given a relation R, for each pair of users u_1 and u_2, such that u_2 grants u_1 some privileges on R, Sysauth contains at most two tuples, one referring to the privileges u_2 grants u_1 with the grant option, and the other referring to the privileges u_2 grants u_1 without the grant option.

Note that Sysauth records whether a user has the update privilege on a relation, but it does not store information on the columns over which the privilege can be exercised (see, for instance, the 4th row of the catalog in Figure 2.2). Such information are stored into Syscolauth. More precisely, Syscolauth stores a tuple: (user, rel, attr, grantor, grantopt) for each attribute attr of relation rel that user can update due to an authorization received from grantor. Attribute grantopt records whether the update privilege is grantable or not. For instance, given the Sysauth catalog in Figure 2.2, Syscolauth will contain the tuple (Marc, Customers, phone, Leo, N).

2.2.4   AUTHORIZATION MANAGEMENT AND ENFORCEMENT

Catalogs Sysauth and Syscolauth are checked by the system to (a) enforce access control; and (b) decide the result of a GRANT/REVOKE command. Access control enforcement is conceptually very easy; verifying whether an access request can be authorized or not can be done simply by querying Sysauth and Syscolauth. For access control enforcement both grantable and non-grantable privileges are considered.

In contrast, to decide the result of a GRANT command only the grantable privileges should be taken into account. Let us see the steps to be performed. First of all, Sysauth and Syscolauth are queried to check whether the user who issues the command has the right of granting the specified privileges. To perform this check, the intersection between the privileges in the GRANT command and the grantable privileges held by the user is performed. Note that grantable privileges can be easily retrieved from Sysauth and Syscolauth by selecting those tuples with grantopt ='Y'. Three different results are possible. If the intersection is empty, than the command is not executed since the user does not have the right to grant any of the privileges in the GRANT command. If the intersection is equal to the privileges listed in the command, than the command is fully executed. Otherwise, the command is partially executed and, as a result, only the privileges in the intersection of the two sets are granted.

Example 2.6   Let us consider the Sysauth and Syscolauth catalogs described above, and the following GRANT commands:

```
Marc: GRANT update(phone) ON Customers TO Robert;
Leo: GRANT delete ON Customers TO John, Ann;
Beth: GRANT select, insert ON Videos TO Alice;
```

The first command is not executed since, according to the information in Sysauth and Syscolauth, Marc holds the update privilege on the phone attribute of the Customers relation but without the grant option. The second command is fully executed since Leo is the owner of the Customers relation. Finally, the last command is partially executed; Beth holds the select privilege on the Videos relation with grant option, whereas she holds the insert privilege without grant option. As such, the result of the command execution is that Alice only receives the select privilege on Videos.

Authorization revocation can be performed only by the user that previously granted the privilege being revoked. Even in this case, verifying whether a user has the right of issuing a REVOKE command requires to simply querying Sysauth and Syscolauth. However, since a user may grant a privilege on a relation not only because he/she is the relation owner but also because he/she has received that privilege with the grant option, what happens to the authorizations granted by a user must be further determined when the privileges he/she used to grant the authorizations are revoked. This is the topic of the following section.

2.2.5   RECURSIVE REVOCATION

Interesting issues are related to the semantics of the revoke operation, since, because of the grant option, more users can be authorized to grant the same privilege on the same relation. The issue to be considered is the following. Suppose there are three users, u_1, u_2, and u_3, and that u_1 grants u_2 privilege p on relation rel with the grant option. Later on, suppose that u_2 grants u_3 privilege p on rel. Moreover, suppose that, after some time, u_1 revokes u_2 p on rel. What happens to the authorization u_2 granted to u_3? The System R access control model enforces *recursive revocation*. This means that whenever a user revokes an authorization on a relation from another user, all the authorizations that the revokee had granted because of the revoked authorization are removed from the authorization state. The revocation is iteratively applied to all the users that received an authorization for the revoked privilege from the revokee.

More formally, the semantics of the revoke operation is captured by the following definition.

Definition 2.7   **(Recursive revoke)** Let $G_1, \ldots, G_n$ be a sequence of GRANT commands, all granting the same privilege on the same relation, such that, if $i < j, 1 \leq i, j \leq n$, then command G_i has been executed before G_j. Let R_i be the REVOKE command revoking the privilege granted by G_i. The semantics of recursive revoke requires that the authorization state after the execution of the sequence of commands:

$$G_1, \ldots, G_n, R_i$$

is equal to the state that one would have after the execution of the sequence of commands:

$$G_1, \ldots, G_{i-1}, G_{i+1}, \ldots, G_n.$$

Therefore, to correctly enforce recursive revocation it is important to remove from the system all the effects of the revoked authorization, that is, all the authorizations that were not grantable if the revoked authorization would not have been specified. The problem can be better modeled and understood by representing the authorization state as a graph, called *authorization graph*. An authorization graph models the state of the authorizations with respect to a specific privilege p and a relation *rel*. The authorization graph contains a node for each user that holds p on *rel*. There is an arc going from node u_1 to node u_2, if u_1 granted p on *rel* to u_2. The arc is labeled with the authorization timestamp and with symbol 'g' if the privilege has been granted with the grant option. The graph always contains a node corresponding to the relation owner since, at the beginning, he/she is the only one that can grant privileges on the relation. Figure 2.3(a) depicts the authorization graph referring to the select privilege and the Videos relation, representing the authorization state corresponding to the Sysauth catalog of Figure 2.2.

Example 2.8   Consider Figure 2.3(a), and suppose that Leo revokes the select privilege on the Videos relation to Gena. This entails the revocation of the select privilege granted by Gena to Matt on relation Videos, since this privilege has been specified only thanks to the authorization Gena received from Leo.

Timestamps are fundamental to correctly enforce recursive revocation, as the following example shows.

Example 2.9   Consider the authorization graph in Figure 2.3(b), referring to the select privilege and the Videos relation, and suppose that Leo revokes the select privilege on Videos to Gena. This does not cause the revocation of the select privilege granted by Gena to Matt on Videos, since this privilege could have been granted by Gena at time 50 even without the privilege being revoked. Indeed, Gena received from Bett the select privilege on Videos at time 40 with the grant option. The result of the revoke operation would be different if the timestamp of the authorization

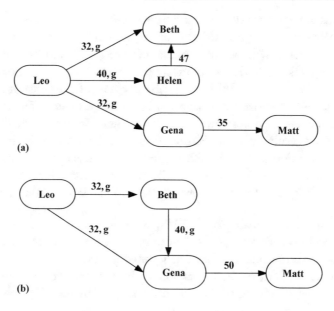

Figure 2.3: Examples of authorization graphs.

granted by Beth to Gena would be greater than 50. In such a case, the revoke operation issued by Leo would entail also the revocation of the privilege granted by Gena to Matt, since this privilege could not have been granted if Gena would not have received the authorization from Leo.

Recursive revocation has the advantage of a well-defined semantics and of being the most conservative solution with respect to data protection. These are the main reasons why it has been implemented by almost all commercial relational DMSs. However, the drawback of such a revoke operation is that it is too disruptive in same cases. For instance, if we consider the example of an organization, the authorizations a user possesses are usually related to his/her particular role within the organization. If a user changes his/her tasks (for instance, because of a promotion), it is desirable to remove only the authorizations of the user, without revoking all the authorizations granted by this user, as recursive revocation would entail. To overcome such limitations, alternative semantics for the revoke operation have been proposed. For instance, *noncascading revocation* has been proposed by Bertino et al. [1997]. This revoke operation differs from recursive revocation in that no recursive revocation is performed upon the execution of a revoke request. In contrast, whenever a user revokes a privilege on a relation from another user, all the authorizations the user may have granted by using the privilege received by the revoker are restated as if they had been granted by the revoker. Then, recursive revocation is applied to the resulting state.

The limitations of recursive revocation have also been recognized by the SQL standard that, starting from SQL:1999, implements a variation of the System R recursive revocation. In SQL, the revoke command can be issued with two options, namely RESTRICT and CASCADE. If the RESTRICT option is specified, the revoke operation is not executed if it entails the revocation of other authorizations or the deletions of some objects from the database schema. In contrast, if the CASCADE option is specified, a variation of recursive revocation is implemented. The difference with the original formulation of System R is that timestamps are not considered to decide whether an authorization should be revoked. As a result, an authorization A granted by a user u is not removed from the system, if, upon the execution of the REVOKE command, u still has an authorization A' granting him/her the right to specify A, regardless of the relations between the timestamps of A' and A. The following example clarifies the differences between the two revoke operations.

Example 2.10 Let us consider again Figure 2.3(b) and suppose that Beth has granted the select privilege with grant option on Videos to Gena at time 55, instead of at time 40. Moreover, suppose that Leo revokes Gena's authorization that was granted at time 32. According to the semantics of recursive revocation, this implies the revocation of the authorization granted by Gena to Matt since $50 < 55$. In contrast, according to the semantics adopted by the SQL cascade revocation, the privilege granted by Gena to Matt is not revoked, because of the privilege granted her by Beth at time 55.

2.2.6 AUTHORIZATIONS ON VIEWS

Views are a key components of any relational DMS and are also the mechanism used by the System R access control model to implement more expressive form of access control with respect to the ones explained so far. For instance, a very important requirement in many environments is to be able to enforce *fine-grained access control*, that is, different protection requirements at a fine granularity level. In the relational data model, this means, for instance, being able to enforce different authorizations on the various attributes in a relation (e.g., the attribute storing the salary of an employee is more sensitive than the attribute name and therefore should be accessed by a restricted number of users). The syntax of the GRANT command presented in Section 2.2.1 does not allow one to specify an authorization which applies only to selected attributes within a relation, with the only exception of the update privilege. Another important requirement is to be able to support *content-dependent* access control (cfr. Chapter 1). In a relational database, this means the ability of authorizing a user to access only selected tuples within a relation, where selection conditions are in terms of attribute values. Furthermore, it is often the case that raw data are very sensitive, whereas aggregate data are less sensitive and, as such, they can be accessible to a wider set of users. For instance, a user can be authorized to see how many videos each customer has rented per month, but he/she should not be allowed to see the titles of these videos. All these requirements cannot be supported through the GRANT command provided by the System R access control model. However, the mechanism to support them is through the use of views. The idea is simple: define a view containing the information the user is authorized to see and then authorize the user to access the view, instead of the base relation(s) over which the view has been built. The query defining the view may contain only selected attributes of a relation, it may select only some tuples of a relation based on the values of some of its attributes, or it may perform aggregate functions on the tuples stored into a relation. Therefore, views can be used to enforce all the protection requirements discussed above. For instance, if we want to authorize a user to access only the information about comedies, we first define a view over Movies where the query in the CREATE VIEW command selects only those tuples whose type attribute is equal to comedy. Then, the user is given access to the view instead of to Movies. A similar approach can be used to give a user access only to aggregate information or only to selected attributes within a relation.

Views are therefore a powerful means with respect to access control. However, we need to pay attention to some aspects related to their management. First of all, a user can create a view only if he/she has the select privilege over the views/relations appearing in its definition. Then, it must be determined which privileges the creator of a view has over it. For base relations, we have seen at the beginning of Section 2.2, that the creator of a relation has all the privileges over it as well as the right to delegate authorization administration to others. For views, this is not true anymore since the privileges a user holds over a created view V depend on two factors: *(1)* the authorizations the user holds over the relations/views over which V has been defined;*(2)* the semantics of the view, that is, its definition in terms of other relations/views. Let us first consider point *(1)*. If a view is defined in terms of a single relation (or view), than the privileges that the creator has on the view are potentially all those he/she holds on the relation/view appearing in the CREATE VIEW command. If the view is defined in terms of more than one relation/view, the privileges over the view are potentially all those obtained by intersecting the privileges the user has on each view/relation appearing in the CREATE VIEW command. Moreover, a privilege on a view is grantable only if the user holds this privilege with the grant option on each view/relation appearing in the CREATE VIEW command. As far as point *(2)* is concerned, it is well known that the SQL standard [ISO, 2003] puts some restrictions on the set of commands executable on a view. The rationale behind these restrictions is that it is not allowed to perform on a view operations that are not unequivocally mappable to the base relations over which the view has been defined. These restrictions may clearly reduce the set of privileges the creator of a view can exercise over it. Therefore, the authorizations a user may potentially exercise on a view according to the rules explained above, are really executable on the view *only if* the execution of these privileges is allowed by the restrictions posed by SQL on the operations that can be performed on views.

Example 2.11   Consider the Sysauth catalog of Figure 2.2, and suppose that Helen executes the following command:

```
CREATE VIEW Comedies AS
SELECT *
FROM Movies
WHERE type = 'comedy';
```

The execution of this command is authorized, since Helen has the `select` privilege on `Movies`. According to the `Sysauth` catalog of Figure 2.2, Helen has also the `update` and `insert` privilege on `Movies`. Such privileges can be exercised by Helen also on the newly created view because no restrictions on the operations that can be performed on it are posed by SQL. Since, the privileges on `Movies` have been granted to Helen with the grant option, she can authorize other users to exercise them on `Comedies`.

Suppose now that the database of the video library contains a further relation `Rentals`, owned by Helen, storing information on the videos rented by the video library customers. Moreover, suppose that Helen creates the view `Rental_Number` that contains the number of rented videos for each customer, as follows:

```
CREATE VIEW Rental_Number AS
SELECT customer, COUNT(*) AS rental_num
FROM Rentals
GROUP_BY customer;
```

Consider, for simplicity, the `select`, `insert`, and `update` privileges only. Since Helen is the creator of the `Rentals` relation, she has the `select`, `insert`, and `update` privileges on it with grant option. These privileges are, in principle, inherited by Helen also on the view, unless they are prevented by the restrictions imposed by SQL on the operations that can be performed over views. These restrictions do not allow one to perform update and insert operations over `Rental_Number`. As a result, Helen can only query the created view and give others such privilege.

Granting and revoking privileges on a view is very similar to the same operations over base relations. You can grant a privilege on a view only if you hold it on the view with the grant option. The revoke operation is recursive. Additionally, when users are allowed to create views it may happen that revocation of a `select` privilege (either over a view or a relation) causes the deletion of one or more views, that is, all the views that have been defined because of the revoked privilege.

Example 2.12 Let us consider the views of Example 2.11 and the `Sysauth` catalog of Figure 2.2, and suppose that Leo revokes from Helen the `select` privilege on `Movies`. As a side effect, the view `Comedies` is deleted, since Helen was allowed to create the view only because of the `select` privilege granted by Leo. Suppose now that Beth creates the following view that counts the number of available videos for each movie offered by the video library:

```
CREATE VIEW HowManyVideos AS
SELECT movie_id, COUNT(*) AS video_num
FROM Videos
GROUP_BY movie_id;
```

Suppose now that Leo revokes from Beth the `select` privilege on `Videos`. The decision whether to delete or not the view `HowManyVideos` depends on the timestamp of the `CREATE VIEW` command. If the timestamp is greater than 47, the view is not deleted, since Beth received at time 47 the `select` privilege on `Videos` by Helen. In contrast, if the `CREATE VIEW` command has been executed by Beth before time 47, the view is recursively deleted.

2.3   DAC SUPPORT IN SQL

The commands to enforce discretionary access control provided by the SQL standard[3] are mainly based on the System R access control model. The standard provides two basic commands, namely `GRANT` and `REVOKE`, with the same purpose as the analogous commands in the System R access control model. However, there are some relevant differences between the two models, the most important ones are the support for Role-based Access Control (see Chapter 5 for more details) and a different semantics for the revoke operation (see Section 2.2.5). Additionally, SQL adds to the System R access control model a new set of privileges and authorization objects, to reflect the extensions made to the relational data model since the design of System R. For instance, SQL supports the `usage` privilege, to authorize a user to make use of a user-defined data type in the definition of the database schema. Additional privileges provided by SQL are `references`, to allow a subject to use an attribute in the specification of a constraint/assertion; `trigger`, that allows one to specify triggers on a given relation; `under`, that allows one to create sub-types and sub-tables, and `execute`, to allow the execution of a procedure/function. There are some restrictions on the granting of these privileges. For instance, `usage` and `execute` privileges cannot be specified for relations, whereas `trigger` can only apply to base relations. We refer the reader to ISO [2003] for all the details. Other extensions related to the set of supported privileges refer to the `select` and `insert` privileges that, differently from the System R access control model, can also be given on selected attributes of a relation.

In addition to the grant option, the SQL `GRANT` command may contain the *hierarchy option*. This clause can be specified for the `select` privilege only, and it allows one to propagate authorizations from a table to all its sub-tables.

Example 2.13   The following are examples of SQL `GRANT` commands:

```
GRANT usage ON TYPE address TO Gena WITH GRANT OPTION;
GRANT execute ON updateCustomers TO Helen;
GRANT select(name, address), references(customer_id) ON Customers TO Marc;
```

The first command authorizes Gena to use the type `address` to define other schema objects. Moreover, since the privilege is granted with grant option, she can authorize other users to make use of the `address` type in the definition of schema objects. The second command authorizes Helen to run procedure `updateCustomers`, whereas the third command authorizes Marc to query

---

[3]Here and in what follows we refer to the SQL:2003 standard [ISO, 2003].

the `name` and `address` attributes of the `Customers` relation. Additionally, the command authorizes Marc to specify constraints involving attribute `customer_id` of the `Customers` relation.

As far as the `REVOKE` command is concerned, apart from the different semantics for the revocation that we have discussed in Section 2.2.5, the main difference with respect to the analogous command in the System R access control model is that it is possible to revoke only the grant/hierarchy option (through the clauses `GRANT OPTION FOR` and `HIERARCHY OPTION FOR`, respectively), without revoking the corresponding privilege.

Example 2.14   With reference to the `GRANT` commands of Example 2.13, the `REVOKE` command:

```
REVOKE GRANT OPTION FOR usage ON TYPE address FROM Gena;
```

revokes from Gena the authorization to grant other users the right to use the `address` type in the definition of other objects of the database schema. However, Gena still maintains the privilege to use type `address`.

2.4   EXTENSIONS TO THE SYSTEM R ACCESS CONTROL MODEL

Because of its relevance, the System R access control model has been extended along several directions with the aim of enhancing its expressive power and adapt it to the requirements of new application scenarios and/or data models. We have already discussed the proposals for an alternative semantics of the revoke operation (cfr. Section 2.2.5). In what follows, we briefly survey the main additional extensions that have been proposed.

Extensions to the System R access control model can be categorized along many different dimensions. In what follows, we classify them into three main categories:

1. **Extended access control models for relational DMSs**. A lot of research proposals have extended the capabilities of the System R access control model with a variety of features, such as the support for group management [Wilms and Lindsay, 1981], negative authorizations [Bertino et al., 1997], role-based [Sandhu et al., 1996] and task-based authorizations, temporal authorizations [Bertino et al., 1998a], and trust management [De Capitani di Vimercati et al., 2007]. Moreover, the System R access control model has been extended for the distributed DMS System R* [Wilms and Lindsay, 1981], whereas Bertino and Haas [1988] extended it with distributed views. Related to those extensions is the problem of developing appropriate tools and mechanisms to efficiently support those extended models.

2. **Development of access control models for advanced data management systems**, like object-oriented, object-relational, active, multimedia, stream-based, XML/RDF-based DMSs, GIS

(Geographical Information System), and data warehouses. These data management systems are usually characterized by data models richer than the relational model. Therefore, access control models developed for relational DMSs must be properly extended to deal with the additional modeling concepts contained in such advanced data models.

3. **Development of access control models for advanced applications and new environments**, such as Web applications and Web Services, applications in the context of Digital Libraries (DLs), or Workflow Management Systems (WFMSs). More recent developments in this field are the access control models developed for Web 2.0 tools, like for instance those developed for social networks, or access control models developed for location-based services.

A detailed description of all the above-mentioned extensions is out of the scope of this book. In what follows, we briefly survey some of the extensions proposed for relational DMSs. Role-based access control is covered in Chapter 5, whereas in Chapter 3 we review some of the developments in the field of object and XML DMSs. We refer the reader to Bertino and Sandhu [2005]; Ferrari and Thuraisingham [2000] for further research results in the context of advanced data management systems. Finally, some of the most recent developments in the field of discretionary access control for advanced applications and new environments will be discussed in Chapter 6.

2.4.1   POSITIVE AND NEGATIVE AUTHORIZATIONS

Bertino et al. [1997] proposed a new semantics for the revoke operation, and provided the support for *negative authorizations*. The System R access control model, like those of most DMSs, does not allow explicit denials to be expressed. The main drawback of such an approach is that the lack of a given authorization for a given user does not prevent this user from receiving this authorization later on (for instance, by one of the users entitled to authorization administration through the grant option). However, there are situations in which the owner of an object (or one of its administrators) would like to prevent others from authorizing the access to that object to specific users. To cope with these requirements, the System R access control model has been extended with the possibility of specifying explicit denials, modeled through *negative authorizations* [Bertino et al., 1997]. Negative authorizations are also supported by SeaView [Lunt et al., 1990], by means of a special privilege denoted as "null". A subject that has the null privilege on a relation cannot exercise any access on it. Thus, it is not possible to deny a subject only selected privileges on a relation. For instance, it is not possible to authorize a subject to see the tuples in a relation and, at the same time, deny it to write on that relation, whereas this is allowed by the model proposed by Bertino et al. [1997]. The support for negative authorizations has been also proposed for RBAC [Al-Kahtani and Sandhu, 2004] and for different data (e.g., Web resources [Bertino et al., 2009], XML [Bertino et al., 2001b]). The drawback of supporting positive and negative authorizations is that authorization enforcement has to deal with conflicts that happen when a subject has both a positive and a negative authorization for the same privilege on the same object. Conflicts between positive and negative authorizations are solved by Bertino et al. [1997] in the most conservative way, that is, according to the "*denials take precedence*" policy, which implies that, whenever a user has both a positive and a negative authorization on the same object for the same privilege, the user is prevented from accessing the object since the negative authorization takes precedence over the positive one. When objects are hierarchically organized, negative authorizations have a further benefit in that they may be used to specify exceptions to the authorization propagation entailed by the hierarchy and therefore they are a means to reduce the number of authorizations that should be specified. As an example, consider the XML data model and an XML document modeling information about projects. Suppose that all the project elements, apart from one, must be accessed by an employee, say Bob, since the information of this project is strictly confidential. Suppose, moreover, that the organization is currently involved in 1000 projects. If negative authorizations are not supported, then 999 authorizations must be specified for Bob, one for each project he is allowed to access. Suppose now that the system supports positive and negative authorizations and that the "denials take precedence" policy is adopted to solve conflicts between them. In such a case, only two authorizations are needed for Bob: a positive one, specified at the document root level, which propagates by default to all the subelements, and a negative authorization specified for the element corresponding to the project that must be kept reserved.

However, although the denials take precedence, policy has the advantage of being intuitive and offering strong protection guarantees, since denials always prevail, it does not fit all the application domains. For instance, when used in combination with subject or object hierarchies it may happen that less specific negative authorizations (that is, authorizations specified at higher levels in the hierarchy) prevail over more specific positive ones. Therefore, different alternative conflict resolution policies have been proposed, in addition to the denials take precedence one, among which:

- *No conflicts.* The presence of a conflict is prevented. Therefore, whenever a user requires the insertion of a new authorization, the system checks whether this authorization conflicts with other authorizations already present in the system and, in this case, rejects the insertion of the new authorization.

- *Permissions take precedence.* The positive authorization prevails over the negative one.

- *Nothing takes precedence.* Neither the positive nor the negative authorization takes precedence. The final result is equivalent to the case where no authorizations had actually been specified. This policy differs from the no conflicts one in that it allows the presence of conflicting authorizations. However, the simultaneous presence of two conflicting authorizations invalidates both of them.

- *Most specific takes precedence.* This policy applies when subjects/objects or privileges are hierarchically organized. In this case, the authorization that is more specific with respect to one of the hierarchies prevails.

- *Priority driven.* Authorizations are associated with a priority level. The authorization with the highest priority prevails.

- *Strong/weak.* Authorizations are classified into strong and weak, and this drives how conflicts are solved. Strong authorizations always override weak ones. Conflicts among strong authorizations are solved according to the no conflicts policy, whereas conflicts among weak authorizations are solved according to the nothing takes precedence policy.

Note, moreover, that the application of only one of this conflict resolution policies may not allow one to decide what authorization prevails. For instance, consider a domain where subjects and objects are hierarchically organized and consider two authorizations (Bob,read,reports,+) and (Manager,read,r_1,-)[4], where reports is a directory containing all the project reports, whereas r_1 is one of them. Now suppose that Bob is a manager requiring to read r_1 and that the most specific takes precedence policy is adopted for conflict resolution. If we consider the object hierarchy the negative authorization prevails, whereas according to the subject hierarchy the positive one wins. Therefore, a further conflict resolution policy is needed, such as one assigning a priority to the various hierarchies [Bertino et al., 2009].

As it is clear from this simple example, different approaches can be taken to deal with conflicts among positive and negative authorizations and the more features the model supports (e.g., hierarchies) the more complex is to deal with conflicts. Additionally, there is no solution that fits all the environments. For this reason, some approaches have been proposed (e.g., Bertino et al. [2003]; Jajodia et al. [2001]) with the aim of providing a flexible framework able to support multiple conflict resolution policies to be customized according to the environment. The importance of supporting negative authorizations has also been recognized by commercial DMSs. For instance, Microsoft SQL Server provides, in addition to the GRANT and REVOKE commands, the DENY command to be used for the specification of negative authorizations.

2.4.2 TEMPORAL AUTHORIZATIONS

A further extension that has been proposed to the System R access control model is the possibility of attaching a validity period to authorizations [Bertino et al., 1998a]. Traditional authorizations are valid from the time they are entered into the system, until they are explicitly removed. However, there are many application scenarios where permissions should be constrained to specific time intervals or periods. An example of policy with temporal constraints is the following: "Programmers can modify the project files every working day except Friday afternoons", because on Friday afternoon a review of the weekly activities is performed. To cope with these requirements, temporal interval can be attached to every authorization representing the time instants in which the authorization is valid [Bertino et al., 1998a]. When the interval expires, the authorization is automatically revoked. The interval associated with an authorization may also be periodic, thus consisting of several intervals that are repeated in time. In addition, the model provides deductive temporal rules to derive new authorizations based on the presence or absence of other authorizations in specific periods of time. For instance, it is possible to specify that two users must be authorized to access an object in the

---

[4]When positive and negative authorizations are supported, the basic format of authorizations described in Chapter 1 is extended with a further component, i.e., the sign, stating whether the authorization is positive (sign = '+') or negative (sign = '-').

same time periods or that a user must be authorized to access an object each time another user does not have this right. The periodic access control model proposed by Bertino et al. [1998a] has been extended by Bertino et al. [2000a] to deal with heterogeneous, distributed systems and with the support for subject and object hierarchies.

Different temporal constraints can be specified through the model defined by Atluri and Gal [2002]. The model which has not been defined for the protection of relational DMSs, but rather for information portals, allows one to specify authorizations, based on the temporal attributes associated with data (such as transaction time and valid time). By this model, it is, for instance, possible to implement a policy authorizing a user to read an object one week after it has been written.

2.5 ORACLE VIRTUAL PRIVATE DATABASE

Oracle Virtual Private Database (VPD) [Oracle Corporation, 2009] is, up to now, one of the most powerful tools supported by commercial DMSs, with the aim of enhancing and simplifying the specification of complex discretionary access control policies. VPD is provided by Oracle starting from version 8i. Main features of Oracle VPD are the support for:

- *fine-grained content-based access control.* An access control policy (i.e., a *policy function*) can be attached directly on a relation/view providing access only to selected tuples (row-level security) or attributes. Tuples authorized by the policy may be selected on the basis of their content.

- *context-dependent access control.* The support for *application contexts* makes it possible to define context-based access control policies (cfr. Chapter 1), that is, policies that depend on some attributes of the session issuing the access request (e.g., IP address, host name) and/or on some characteristics of the profile of the subject issuing the request (e.g., whether the user is a database administrator).

One of the main advantages of VPD is its increased flexibility in terms of supported access control requirements. For instance, by using the access control support provided by SQL, the only way to enforce context-based access control is to embed the access control checks into application programs. VPD provides better security with respect to this solution, since policies are server-enforced and therefore they are checked whatever is the application accessing the database. Additionally, VPD achieves better scalability, since the support for fine-grained, content-based access control does not require the management of a huge number of views. As an example, consider once again the video library database and suppose we would like to enforce a policy stating that each customer can access information only on his/her rentals. Enforcing this policy using the support provided by SQL requires the generation of a number of views equal to the number of customers of the video library. Using VPD, enforcing the same policy requires the generation of only one *policy function* and its attachment to the Rentals relation. This also makes policy specification easier.

Let us now see how VPD works. First of all, a function coding the access control policy to be enforced must be specified and attached to the object being protected. Objects can be relations, views, or synonyms. The policy function returns a predicate encoding the access control checks implied by the policy. When a user accesses an object protected by a policy function, the issued SQL statement is dynamically modified by the Oracle DMS. This modification is transparent to the user and creates a WHERE condition containing the predicate(s) returned by the attached policy function(s). Then, the modified query is executed and the results returned to the user.

VPD functions may exploit *application contexts*. An application context stores a set of properties of users/sessions that may be used by VPD policies to enforce context-based access control constraints. Application contexts may be system or user defined. Oracle provides a default context, namely USERENV, that contains a set of properties of user sessions (such as user id, IP address, host name, etc.). Attributes of the USERENV context cannot be modified. If one wants to specify a policy exploiting additional attributes with respect to those contained into USERENV, he/she can create his/her own contexts, through the CREATE CONTEXT command. To create a context a user must be granted the CREATE ANY CONTEXT system privilege. Context attributes may be queried through the command:

```
SYS_CONTEXT (<namespace>,<attribute>);
```

where: <namespace> is the name of the application context to be queried, and <attribute> is one of its attributes.

Attributes of user-defined contexts may be modified through the following command:

```
DBMS_SESSION.SET_CONTEXT(<namespace>,<attribute>,<value>);
```

Example 2.15   Let us consider the policy described above, authorizing each customer to access only his/her rentals. Moreover, suppose that Admin can access the rentals of any customer and let us see how the policy can be implemented using VPD. In this case, it is not necessary to create a context since all the information needed to enforce this policy can be found in the USERENV context. Therefore, the first step is to create a policy function. This can be done as follows:

```
CREATE FUNCTION check_access (p_schema VARCHAR2, p_obj VARCHAR2)
RETURN VARCHAR2 AS user VARCHAR2(100);
BEGIN
  IF( SYS_CONTEXT('USERENV', 'ISDBA') ) THEN
    RETURN ' ';
  ELSE
      user := SYS_CONTEXT('USERENV', 'SESSION_USER');
      RETURN 'customer =' || user;
  END IF;
END;
```

where the parameters of the policy function denote the schema and the object (table, view, synonym) over which the function is invoked. Then, a VPD policy invoking the newly created policy function

video	customer	rental_date	return_date
1245	Leo	2-12-2009	2-14-2009
1374	Ann	8-1-2010	8-1-2010
1374	Leo	5-3-2010	5-4-2010
1521	Alice	4-16-2010	null

Figure 2.4: Rentals relation.

should be attached to the Rentals relation. This can be done through the ADD_POLICY procedure, as follows[5]:

```
DBMS_RLS.ADD_POLICY ( object_schema => 'VideoLibrary',
                      object_name => 'Rentals',
                      policy_name => 'secure_access',
                      policy_function => 'check_access',
                      statement_types => 'select, update, insert');
```

where statement_types lists the SQL commands for which the policy should be enforced. Now suppose that Ann issues the following SQL command:

```
SELECT * FROM Rentals;
```

The query is rewritten by attaching a WHERE clause having as predicate the result of check_access, that is:

```
SELECT * FROM Rentals WHERE customer = 'Ann';
```

VPD policies can also be based on user-defined contexts. To create a user-defined context, the first step is to create a PL/SQL package that sets the attributes of the context. Then, through the CREATE CONTEXT command, it is possible to create a namespace for the new application context and associate it with the PL/SQL package.

VDP also supports *column-level* policies, that is, policies that are evaluated only when selected columns are referenced either directly or indirectly in a query. If a VPD column-level policy is specified for a column C of a relation R, then, when C is referenced in a query, the system returns by default only the rows of R that satisfy the policy. Columns that trigger the evaluation of the policy can be specified by using the sec_relevant_cols parameter of the ADD_POLICY procedure.

Example 2.16   Consider the relation in Figure 2.4 and suppose that the following policy should be enforced over it: each user can see all the information in the Rentals relation, apart from information

[5]We refer the interested readers to Oracle Corporation [2009] for the whole list of parameters that can be used in the ADD_POLICY procedure.

on the rented videos, in that each user can access only his/her own video information. Such policy can be easily implemented through a column-level VPD policy as follows. First of all, a policy function is created implementing the required checks:

```
CREATE FUNCTION check_access_video ( p_schema VARCHAR2,
                                     p_obj VARCHAR2)
RETURN VARCHAR2 AS user VARCHAR2(100);
BEGIN
    user := SYS_CONTEXT('USERENV', 'SESSION_USER');
    RETURN 'customer =' || user;
END;
```

Then, the policy function is attached to Rentals:

```
DBMS_RLS.ADD_POLICY (object_schema => 'VideoLibrary',
                     object_name => 'Rentals',
                     policy_name => 'secure_access_video',
                     policy_function => 'check_access_video',
                     sec_relevant_cols => 'video');
```

The access control policy applies when the columns listed in the sec_relevant_cols parameter are referenced, explicitly or implicitly, in a query.

Now suppose that Leo issues the following query:

Q$_1$: SELECT customer, rental_date FROM Rentals;

In such a case, the policy secure_access_video is not evaluated since the query does not reference attribute video. As a result, the query is executed as it is, and the result returned to Leo is the one in Figure 2.5(a). In contrast, suppose that Leo issues the following query:

Q$_2$: SELECT video, rental_date FROM Rentals;

In such a case, the secure_access_video policy is enforced and the query is rewritten as follows:

```
SELECT video, rental_date FROM Rentals WHERE customer = 'Leo';
```

The result returned to Leo is the relation shown in Figure 2.5(b).

Finally, it is also possible to request a *masking behavior* with respect to the enforcement of column-level policies. In this case, all the rows satisfying the query are returned, but a null value is displayed for the columns to which the policy refers to, if the corresponding value does not satisfy the policy. For instance, consider the queries in Example 2.16 and suppose that the masking behavior has been required instead of the default one. The result of query Q$_1$ does not change, whereas the new result for query Q$_2$ is shown in Figure 2.6.

customer	rental_date
Leo	2-12-2009
Ann	8-1-2010
Leo	5-3-2010
Alice	4-16-2010

(a)

video	rental_date
1245	2-12-2009
1374	5-3-2010

(b)

Figure 2.5: Examples of column-level policy enforcement.

video	rental_date
1245	2-12-2009
null	8-1-2010
1374	5-3-2010
null	4-16-2010

Figure 2.6: Masking behavior.

To obtain the masking behavior, it is necessary to set the `sec_relevant_cols_opt` parameter of the `DBMS_RLS.ADD_POLICY` procedure to `DBMS_RLS.ALL_ROWS`. There are a number of restrictions for the application of the column-masking behavior, such as that it can apply only to `SELECT` statement, and the result of the invocation of the policy function should be a simple Boolean expression.

Views/tables and synonyms can be protected by multiple policies. When several policies are attached to a schema object, they are enforced with the AND syntax. This means that they need to be *all* satisfied to get access. This is different from the approach enforced by the System R access control model and SQL, where policies are enforced with the OR syntax (that is, the privileges a user can exercise are the union of those he/she receives through different `GRANT` commands). Finally, policies can be deleted by invoking `DBMS_RLS.DROP_POLICY`, whereas `DBMS_RLS.ENABLE_POLICY` can be used to temporarily enable a previously specified policy.

Note that there are two classes of users that by-pass VPD policies. The first is `SYS` users, which are exempt by default by VPD policies. Additionally, it is also possible to authorize other users to by-pass the checks of VPD policies, by granting them the EXEMPT ACCESS POLICY system privilege.

A VPD policy function runs by default as if it had been declared with definer's rights, that is, it executes with the privileges of its owner, not of its current user. For better security, the Oracle guide recommends not to declare it as invoker's rights.

In conclusion, VPD provides a very powerful tool to specify access control policies without the need for coding their logic into application programs outside the DMS and, up to now, it is the only example of this type of advanced tools provided by commercial DMSs. However, because of the expressive power and the flexibility it provides, it may be very difficult to verify whether or not a particular user has the right to access a particular object in a particular state. Therefore, VPD policies must be used by trading-off the complexity of the requirements one would like to enforce and the possibility of easily determining the authorization state.

Moreover, VPD query rewriting may, in same cases, cause inconsistencies between what the user requires and what the system returns [Rizvi et al., 2004], as the following example shows.

Example 2.17   Consider again the policy authorizing each customer to see only his/her rentals. Suppose that a customer, say Ann, issues the following query to know how many videos have been rented in the video library:

```
SELECT COUNT(*) FROM Rentals;
```

Because of the VPD policy defined over Rentals the query is rewritten as follows:

```
SELECT COUNT(*) FROM Rentals WHERE customer = 'Ann';
```

giving Ann the impression that the numbers of rented videos is equal to the number of videos she rent. Moreover, suppose that Ann issues a query to find all the customers who have rented more videos than her. Because of the VPD policy, the query does not return any tuple.

VPD query rewriting belongs to the class of models, referred to as *Truman models* [Rizvi et al., 2004]. In a Truman model, each user has a personal and restricted view of the database (in Oracle VPD, the view is determined by the evaluation of the defined policy functions). User queries are then modified transparently to avoid that the user accesses anything outside his/her view of the database. However, as shown by Example 2.17, this may result in misleading query answers, in some cases. An alternative approach is the non-Truman model [Rizvi et al., 2004]. Under the non-Truman model, a query undergoes a validity test, and only if the validity test succeeds it is executed, it is rejected, otherwise. If the query passes the test, than it is executed without modification. The problem is how to define the validity of a query and how to test for it. The risk is that a lot of queries are not executed because they do not pass the validity test.

CHAPTER 3

Discretionary Access Control for Advanced Data Models

In Chapter 2, we surveyed discretionary access control models developed for relational data management systems. New developments in the field of Discretionary Access Control (DAC) have been determined by the evolution in the data models adopted by data management systems. In this chapter, we discuss the access control models proposed for the object and the XML data models. These data models are semantically richer than the relational one, and therefore their protection requires an extension to the models proposed for relational data.

3.1 ACCESS CONTROL FOR OBJECT DMSs

Access control models developed for relational DMSs should be redesigned when dealing with object-oriented and, recently, object-relational DMSs (in what follows, we will refer to both kind of systems as object data management systems—ODMSs for short) because of the deep differences in the underlying data model. The main difference between the relational model and the object one is that relations are a flat structure, whereas classes in the object data model may be hierarchically organized. Moreover, the object model is characterized by semantic modeling concepts such as those of composite objects and versions that are not present in the relational data model. Such modeling concepts need to be taken into account when developing an access control model. For instance, the semantic relationships existing in the object model can be exploited to establish relationships between the authorizations given on semantically related objects. The other key difference between the object model and the relational one is that an object, besides being a data container, can have methods associated with it. Therefore, method invocation and their accesses to the managed data should be properly regulated.

The most comprehensive access control model developed for ODMSs is the one developed for the Orion DMS [Rabitti et al., 1991]. The Orion access control model offers a variety of features, such as the support for positive and negative authorizations, as well as weak and strong authorizations (cfr. Section 2.4.1). Authorizations are granted to roles instead of to single users. Roles form a rooted directed acyclic graph called *role lattice*. Roles, objects, and privileges are organized into hierarchies to which a set of propagation rules apply. Propagation rules along the role hierarchy allow the derivation of implicit authorizations, according to the following criteria: 1) if a role has an authorization to access an object, all the roles preceding it in the role hierarchy have the same authorization; 2) if a role has a negative authorization to access an object, all the roles that follow it in the role hierarchy have the same negative authorization. Similar propagation rules are defined for privileges. Finally, propagation rules on objects allow authorizations on an object to be derived from the authorizations on objects semantically related to it. For example, the authorization to read a class implies the authorization to read all its instances. A consistency condition is defined on propagation rules, which requires that, given a weak or strong authorization, the application of the propagation rules supported by the model to the authorization does not generate conflicting authorizations. Further extensions to the Orion access control model have been proposed by Bertino and Weigand [1994], such as, the definition of new authorization types and the revisiting of some propagation rules. The model has been further extended by Bertino et al. [2000b] along different directions: the support for both roles and groups with a clear functional distinction between them, the possibility of granting authorizations to single user and not only to roles; the support for user-defined derivation rules to derive implicit authorizations not only along the role, object, and privilege hierarchies, like in the Orion access control model. Another difference is related to the concept of strong and weak authorizations. In the Orion model, strong authorizations cannot be overridden. This implies that the insertion of a strong authorization is rejected by the system if it conflicts with an existing strong authorization. This clearly prevents strong authorizations to be granted through derivation rules. To allow strong authorizations to be derived through derivation rules, an approach has been proposed that allows strong authorizations to be overridden by other positive or negative strong authorizations.

Another relevant proposal is the access control model developed for Iris [Ahad et al., 1992]. The distinguishing feature of this model with respect to the Orion access control model is that it considers methods as authorization objects. More precisely, in Iris both attributes and methods are represented as functions. Therefore, the only privilege supported by the model is the call privilege, that authorizes a subject to call a function. The call privilege can be granted or revoked both on a per-group and on a per-user basis. A user can belong to several groups and groups can be nested. Similar to the System R access control model, the creator of a function is the owner of the function and automatically receives the call privilege on it as well as the authorization to grant other subjects the call privilege on the function. Call privileges can be granted with the grant option, therefore making the user receiving the privilege able to grant others the received call privilege.

Functions can also be defined in terms of other functions. In such a case, they are called derived functions. The protection of derived functions can be managed under two different approaches. Under the first, called *static authorization*, the subject requesting the execution of a derived function must have the call privilege only on the derived function. The second mode, called *dynamic authorization*, is more restrictive since it requires that the caller must have the call privilege both on the derived function and on all the functions that are executed by the derived function. The protection mode is specified by the creator of the derived function. To provide a better control over a function invocation, the Iris access control model provides two novel constructs: *guard* and *proxy* functions. Guard functions allow one to express preconditions on the call of a function and are therefore used to restrict the access to a given function and to enforce content-based access control. The function to which a guard function refers to is called the target function. A target function is executed only if the corresponding guard function is evaluated successfully. Conditions are imposed to guarantee that the evaluation of guards will terminate. The main advantage of guard functions is that they restrict the access to a function without requiring changes to the function code. Proxy functions provide different implementations of a specific function for different subjects (or groups of subjects). When a function is invoked, the appropriate proxy function is executed instead of the original one.

We are not aware of access control models specifically developed for object-relational data management systems, however some of the ideas developed for object-oriented data management systems can be applied to the object-relational model as well. For instance, object-relational data management systems provide methods associated with user-defined types. Methods are therefore objects to be protected, like in an object-oriented data management system.

3.2   ACCESS CONTROL FOR XML DATA

XML [Bray et al., 2004] is the standard today for modeling and transmitting data on the Web and one of the key technologies of the Semantic Web.

The most important characteristic of XML, that distinguishes it from other markup languages, such as HTML, is the notion of *semantic tags*, allowing one to structure a document into different portions, called *elements*, with an associated semantics. An element may also contain attributes, whose purpose is to provide additional information on the element. XML documents may have a nested or hierarchical structure, since elements can be organized into sub-elements; they may be inter-linked, through IDREFs/URI attributes; they may have an associated DTD/XMLSchema, specifying their structures. A DTD/XMLSchema is a concept closely related to that of relation schema or class, in that it is used to intensionally describe the structure of a set of XML documents. However, unlike relational data, XML documents are not always instances of a DTD/XMLSchema. The term *valid* XML document is used to denote those XML documents which are instances of some DTD/XMLSchema.

Because of the relevance of XML, a lot of effort has been spent in addressing its security. A set of W3C standards have been defined, such as XML Encryption and XML Signature[1]. As far as access control is concerned, the most relevant standardization effort is the OASIS standard language XACML (eXtensible Access Control Markup Language) [Moses, 2005]. The XACML specification has a twofold goal: *1)* it describes the vocabulary and syntax of the language for expressing access control policies, and *2)* it states the framework to support the access control decision process, based on such a language.

Additionally, a lot of research work has been done towards the development of access control models and mechanisms for XML data. In what follows, we first discuss the main protection requirements of XML data, then we review the literature. Finally, we survey some of the strategies that have been proposed to speed-up access control.

---

[1]http://www.w3.org/.

3.2.1   ACCESS CONTROL REQUIREMENTS

XML documents can be represented as graphs, as shown in Figure 3.1. In the graph representation, white nodes represent elements, whereas gray nodes represent attributes. A node representing an attribute contains its associated value. The graph contains edges representing the element-to-attribute and the element-to-subelement relationships. Edges are labeled with the tag of the destination node (i.e., an element or an attribute) and are represented by solid lines.

As far as access control is concerned, first of all, the nested interlinked structure of XML data calls for a flexible specification of protection objects. Access control should be fine grained in that protection objects can be selected elements/attributes/links within a document (e.g., the attribute salary of the employee element). Additionally, access control policies can also be specified for whole documents, when all their portions have the same protection requirements. Furthermore, data may have an associated intensional description of their structure (i.e., DTD/XMLSchema) and this intensional description should be exploited for policy specification. For example, it must be possible to specify access control policies at the DTD/XMLSchema level, which apply to all valid documents conforming to that DTD/XMLSchema. Moreover, the access control model should also be able to manage documents not conforming to any DTD/XMLSchema.

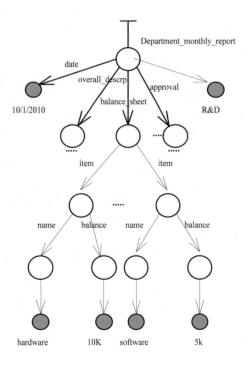

Figure 3.1: An example of XML document.

Besides the variety of granularity levels, a further requirement is the support for content-dependent access control. This is particularly relevant for XML data where elements may contain unstructured text of various length (element data content).

Example 3.1   With reference to the XML document in Figure 3.1, secretaries, managers and accountants working in the R&D department can be entitled to see the information contained in the monthly report of their department, whereas secretaries working in different departments can be entitled to see all the information in the report apart from balance sheet variations. Additionally, the company managing director can be authorized to see the monthly reports of all the company departments (this last requirement can be modeled through a policy specified at the DTD level, which applies to all the monthly report files).

A further requirement derives from the heterogeneous user population accessing the Web. In this context, conventional identity-based access control scheme, where the authorizations a user holds are determined on the basis of his/her id are no more appropriate, in that they can result in a huge number of authorizations to be managed. Moreover, access control decisions are usually based on a set of properties of the user that goes beyond his/her identity. In this context, *credential-based* access control is more appropriate [Biskup and Wortmann, 2004]. A credential (or profile) contains a set of characteristics of a user, which are considered relevant for access control purposes (e.g., age, nationality, membership to some associations). Access control policies may then be specified on the basis of credential properties.

Another important requirement is the support for different dissemination modes for the managed data. Indeed, in the Web, it is worthwhile to be able to support at least two dissemination modes: pull and push. According to a pull dissemination mode, data reside at one or more servers and the subjects ask them when needed, by issuing proper access request(s). This is the dissemination mode usually adopted by commercial DMSs. However, besides the traditional pull mode, also a push dissemination mode can be successfully adopted. Such mode is suitable for documents that must be released to a large community of subjects which show a regular behavior with respect to their release (e.g., they must be periodically distributed or when some pre-defined events happen). According to a push mode, a data management system periodically broadcasts (portions of) its XML documents to authorized subjects, without the need of an explicit access request by a subject.

3.2.2   ACCESS CONTROL MODELS

To protect XML data it is possible to borrow some ideas from the access control models developed in the context of object data management systems (see Section 3.1). For instance, the support for policy propagation from DTD/XMLSchema to their instances, as well as the exploitation of semantic relationships among different portions of an XML document (e.g., element-to-subelements, element-to-attributes) as a further means to propagate authorizations and simplify their management.

Table 3.1: Comparison of discretionary models for XML data

Requirement	[Bertino et al., 2001b]	[Damiani et al., 2002]	[Gabillon and Bruno, 2002]	[Murata et al., 2006]	[Kudo and Hada, 2000]	[Kanza et al., 2006]
Sbj spec.	sbj credentials	sbj ids sbj location, groups	user ids and groups	roles and groups	user ids roles	user ids roles
Obj spec.						
granularity	any element and attribute specified by XPath	any element and attribute specified by XPath	any element and attribute specified by XPath	any element and attribute specified by XPath	any element and attribute specified by XPath	any element and attribute specified by XPath/ relationships
content	yes	yes	yes	yes	yes	yes
intensional	yes	yes	-	yes	yes	-
Access modes	browsing and authoring	read	read	read, update create, delete	read, write create, delete	read
Propagation	implicit and explicit	local and recursive	to subtrees to which policies apply	to subtrees to which policies apply	up and down	-
Exception management	based on sign	based on sign, hard/soft	based on sign	based on sign	based on sign	-
Conflict resolution	most specific takes precedence	denial takes precedence	based on priority	denial takes precedence	denial/permission nothing takes precedence	-
Constraints		-	-	-	prov. actions context-based	context-based

Discretionary access control mechanisms for XML data have been proposed by many researchers and some of them are described in what follows. Nearly all of them use XPath [Melton and Buxton, 2006] to denote protection objects, since through XPath it is possible to provide support for fine-grained and content-based access control. Then, they mainly differ with respect to the requirements they are able to express, how authorization propagation and conflicts are managed, how authorization subjects are specified, and how access control is enforced. Table 3.1 provides a comparative analysis of the presented models. In what follows, we review them by classifying the proposals according to the way they enforce access control.

3.2.2.1   Query Rewriting

In the majority of the access control models for XML data, access control enforcement is based on query rewriting with the aim of pruning from the node set resulting from query evaluation those nodes that a subject is not authorized to access according to the specified access control policies. Models adopting this strategy are also referred to as Truman models (cfr. Section 2.5). Query rewriting is for instance exploited by the model proposed by Damiani et al. [2002] that allows the specification of policies based both on subject identity (i.e., ids), and subject location (i.e., IP addresses), as well as for groups, that are either sets of users, or *location patterns* identifying a set of physical locations. As many other access control models for XML data, the model is quite rich in the types of authorizations that can be specified, in that it provides support for positive and negative authorizations and for soft and hard authorizations. As far as authorization propagation is concerned, different options are possible. Authorizations can be either local or recursive. A local authorization on a document element applies to all the element attributes, but it does not propagate to the sub-elements, whereas this propagation is enacted by recursive authorizations. In contrast, soft authorizations apply to a document, unless an authorization has been specified at the DTD level, whereas hard authorizations are specified at the DTD level and apply to all the DTD instances, with no exceptions.

Another proposal exploiting query rewriting to enforce access control is the model by Gabillon and Bruno [2002] that makes use of XPath to denote the protection objects to which a policy applies. Subject specification can be either in terms of user ids or groups. Policies can be either positive or negative. Explicit propagation is supported, in that if a subject is allowed (or denied) to access a document node n, he/she is automatically allowed (or denied) to access also the sub-tree rooted at n. Access control policies could have an optional *priority* component, which states the importance of the policy in evaluating an access request and therefore is used for conflict resolution between positive and negative authorizations.

The distinguishing feature of the model proposed by Kudo and Hada [2000] is the support for provisional access control. An access request is authorized provided that the requesting subject (and/or the system) performs certain security actions. An example of provisional authorization is: "You are allowed to read sensitive data, but you must sign a terms and conditions statement first" [Kudo and Hada, 2000]. Subjects can be either users or roles. Additionally, the model supports the notion of context, allowing data such as the time and location of the access request to be used in policy specification. The model supports a variety of conflict resolution policies (i.e., denials take precedence, permissions take precedence, and nothing takes precedence) and propagation policies (propagation up and down in the document hierarchy) to be selected when a policy is specified (see Table 3.1).

The most comprehensive solution in the framework of discretionary models for protecting XML documents up to now is the one developed in the framework of the Author-$\mathcal{X}$ system [Bertino and Ferrari, 2002; Bertino et al., 2001b]. Author-$\mathcal{X}$ is a Java-based system enforcing credential-based discretionary access control on XML documents. Author-$\mathcal{X}$ takes into account XML document characteristics, the presence of DTDs/XMLSchemas intensionally describing the structure of documents, and the types of actions that can be executed on XML documents (i.e., authoring and browsing). Authorizations can be either positive or negative. Conflicts are solved according to the "most specific takes precedence" principle (cfr. Section 2.4.1). In particular, access control policies defined for specific documents prevail over those defined for DTDs (because the latter are considered less specific) and policies defined at a lower level in a document or DTD hierarchy prevail over those defined at higher levels. The model supports both implicit and explicit propagation of authorizations. Implicit propagation implies that an authorization specified for a DTD/XMLSchema applies to all the instances, and an authorization specified for an element propagates to all its attributes and links. Exceptions to implicit propagation can be managed by specifying explicit positive and negative authorizations. Additionally, a user may explicitly require the propagation of authorizations from an element to all the direct/indirect sub-elements (CASCADE option), or to the direct sub-elements only (FIRST_LEVEL option), or state that no propagation is enacted (NO_PROP option).

Example 3.2   Figure 3.2 reports the Author-$\mathcal{X}$ policies modeling the protection requirements described in Example 3.1. In Author-$\mathcal{X}$, credentials are expressed in XML and the policy subject specification is an XPath expression on the XML files coding credentials. Note that the requirement that secretaries not working in the R&D department are entitled to see all the information in the report apart from balance sheet variations is modeled by means of two policies: a positive policy on the Department_monthly_report element referring to the R&D department and a negative policy on the balance_sheet element.

However, the distinguishing features of Author-$\mathcal{X}$ are not related to the policy specification language, but rather to the various dissemination modes it provides and to the support for cooperative distributed updates of XML documents. More precisely, Author-$\mathcal{X}$ supports both the pull and push dissemination modes. Pull distribution is based on query rewriting, whereas push distribution is efficiently obtained through the use of encryption techniques: different portions of the same XML document are encrypted with different encryption keys, on the basis of the specified access control policies. Then, the same encrypted copy of the document is distributed to all subjects, whereas each subject receives only the key(s) for the portion(s) he/she is enabled to access. To limit the overhead implied by key management, Author-$\mathcal{X}$ adopts a hierarchical key management

```
<policy_base>
<policy_spec cred_expr="//manager[Department="R&D"]" target="Department_monthly_report.xml"
  path="//Department_monthly_report[@Department="R&D"]" priv="VIEW" type="GRANT"
  prop="CASCADE"/ >
<policy_spec cred_expr="//secretary[Department="R&D"]" target="Department_monthly_report.xml"
  path="//Department_monthly_report[@Department="R&D"]" priv="VIEW" type="GRANT"
  prop="CASCADE"/ >
<policy_spec cred_expr="//accountant[Department="R&D"]" target="Department_monthly_report.xml"
  path="//Department_monthly_report[@Department="R&D"]" priv="VIEW" type="GRANT"
  prop="CASCADE"/ >
<policy_spec cred_expr="//secretary[Department≠"R&D"]" target="Department_monthly_report.xml"
  path="//Department_monthly_report[@Department="R&D"]/balance_sheet" priv="VIEW" type="DENY"
  prop="CASCADE"/ >
<policy_spec cred_expr="//secretary[Department≠"R&D"]" target="Department_monthly_report.xml"
  path="//Department_monthly_report.xml[@Department="R&D"]" priv="VIEW" type="GRANT"
  prop="CASCADE"/ >
<policy_spec cred_expr="//company_managing_director" target="Department_monthly_report.dtd"
  path="" priv="VIEW" type="GRANT" prop="CASCADE"/ >
</policy_base>
```

Figure 3.2: An example of Author-$\mathcal{X}$ policy base.

scheme [Bertino et al., 2002] that requires the permanent storage of a number of keys linear in the number of access control policies.

The other important service provided by Author-$\mathcal{X}$ is the support for distributed cooperative updates. This allows to totally or partially specify, at the beginning of the update process, the path that the document must follow, that is, the subjects that should modify it and the order in which these updates must take place. Then, through a combination of hash functions, digital signature techniques and digital certificates [Mella et al., 2006] each subject receiving the document can: *1)* update the document portions he/she is authorized to modify; and *2)* check the integrity of the document with respect to the update operations performed so far, without interacting with the document server.

The push dissemination mode for XML documents is also addressed by Crampton [2004], where the hierarchical structure of XML documents is exploited to form a hierarchy of permissions, which are then grouped to form roles. Access control enforcement is based on the use of cryptographic techniques, and each role basically corresponds to the keys associated with its permissions.

3.2.2.2   Static Analysis

According to this approach to access control enforcement, authorizations are not checked at run-time, rather they are statically evaluated to decide the result of an access request. Among the proposals in this direction, a static analysis approach based on automata, has been proposed by Murata et al. [2006]. By means of an automata, it is possible to verify whether a query accesses only authorized nodes with respect to the specified access control policies without accessing the XML documents. For those queries that are *statically indeterminate* a further run-time check is needed. The most innovative contribution of this approach is related to the proposed static analysis technique, whereas the underlying access control model is quite standard and subsumed by the already discussed proposals.

Authorization subjects are either roles or groups, whereas protection objects are denoted through XPath. Authorizations (positive and negative) can either propagate downward through the XML document structure, or just apply on the nodes for which they are explicitly specified. Conflicts among positive and negative authorizations are solved in favor of the negative ones.

A non-Truman model for XML data access control has been proposed by Kanza et al. [2006], where a query that violates the specified access control policies is rejected, rather than modified. Query that can be safely answered are called *valid* queries. In this model access control rules are specified through XPath. These rules specify relationships between elements that should be concealed from users. This means that the model is able to protect not only elements but also edges and paths in the XML graph. Different from the other models illustrated so far, authorization rules specify denials, that is, what relationships should be concealed, rather than permissions. Access control rules may be parameterized with context information, such as location, date, time, etc. Although Kanza et al. [2006] did not give a precise definition of which kinds of subjects the model supports, the included examples suggest that the model provides support for roles and users. Two notions of query validity are given. The first is local validity, which requires that, given a document and a query, all relationships protected by the specified access control rules are concealed in the query answer. For queries against documents that conform to an XMLSchema, a stronger notion may be given, that is, global validity. Given a set of access control rules and an XMLSchema, a query is globally valid for the set of rules and the schema if it is locally valid for the rules and each document that conforms to the schema.

3.2.3   EFFICIENCY OF ACCESS CONTROL

Other relevant work in the field of XML access control focus on the efficiency of access control enforcement. Indeed, the fine-grained access control provided by most access control models for XML data, possibly combined with credential-based access control and the huge population accessing the Web, may result in a great overhead for access control, due to the large number of authorizations that must be checked. Therefore, whichever access control model is adopted, it must be equipped with suitable strategies for speeding-up access control. The approaches proposed so far for this purpose may be roughly classified into three groups:

- **View materialization**. The idea of this approach is to define a view for each subject (or subject group), containing all and only the accessible document portions. This approach is, for instance, explored by Fan et al. [2004], where a different view (called security view) is defined for each subject group, which consists of all and only the information accessible to the group according to the specified access control policies. An algorithm is then given to rewrite XPath queries in terms of security views. The main drawback of view-based approaches is the huge number of views that could be potentially generated and maintained.

- **Query pre-processing**. The idea of this approach is to pre-process the subject query to statically determine whether or not it accesses unauthorized document portions. For instance, an approach based on a non-deterministic finite automata has been proposed by Luo et al.

[2004] for checking a user query against access control policies, and defining a new query in such a way that it will return only authorized portions. Another pre-processing approach is the one proposed by Murata et al. [2006], where, by performing a static analysis of the access control policies, the query, and the target XMLSchema, it is possible to classify queries as either authorized or prohibited.

- **Auxiliary data structures**. According to this approach, ad-hoc data structures are defined to speed up access control enforcement. For instance, Yu et al. [2004] defined a compressed accessibility map (CAM) making it easier to determine the XML data item to which a subject has access. An accessibility map is built directly on the XML document for each different subject and access mode, by marking each node with information stating whether or not it is accessible by the subject. A method to reduce the storage space needed for the accessibility map is also defined, which considers the propagation according to which a policy applying to a node is inherited by its children nodes. Qi and Kudo [2005] proposed a tree data structure, called Policy Matching Tree (PMT), that traces each access control policy applied on an XML source. The tree is built by analyzing each access control policy and by inserting a non-leaf node for each test imposed by the object specification of the considered access control policy. The access control policies that match a subject query are all those identified by the paths connecting the root node to a leaf node. The main drawback of this approach is the possible high complexity of the PMT structure when access control policies with complex path expressions are specified. An XML-based structure, called AC-XML document, has been proposed by Carminati and Ferrari [2005]. AC-XML documents are associated with the DTDs/XMLSchemas belonging to the data source being protected, and they keep track of the policies applicable to each portion of the instances of the schema to which they refer to. AC-XML documents are built during a start-up phase of the access control procedure, which incrementally binds policies with protected objects each time a new access request is submitted.

CHAPTER 4

Mandatory Access Control

One of the main advantages of discretionary access control is its flexibility in terms of the access control requirements it can support. Indeed, by properly configuring the authorization state a variety of different confidentiality/integrity requirements can be modeled. This is why DAC has been adopted by most commercial DMSs and supported by the SQL standard. However, the main drawback of DAC is that it does not provide control on the information flow within the system. Indeed, once an authorized subject has gained access to an object, it can pass the information it contains to an unauthorized subject (for instance, by writing such information into another object), without bypassing the checks performed by the reference monitor. This makes DAC vulnerable to malicious attacks, such as *Trojan Horses* embedded in application programs. A Trojan Horse is a malware that appears to perform or actually performs a useful function for the user but, in addition, makes unauthorized accesses to the protected objects possible. The following is an example of a Trojan Horse.

Example 4.1   Suppose that Ann and Paul are both employees of the video library and that Ann is Paul's manager. Moreover, suppose that, according to the access control policies in place in the video library, Ann is authorized to read and modify the content of all the relations in the database, as well as to grant other users access authorizations on them, whereas Paul is not allowed to see the name of the movies rented by the customers of the video library. Now suppose that Paul gives Ann a program for calendar management in which he has maliciously inserted some lines of codes (that is, the Trojan Horse) to get access to the names of the movies rented by the customers of the video library. More precisely, the Trojan Horse performs the following operations (see Figure 4.1): *(i)* it creates a new relation `CustomerMovies` that stores, for each customer, the name of the movies he/she has rented; *(ii)* it grants Paul the `select` privilege on the newly created relation. When Ann executes the program, the reference monitor checks the access/granting requests made by the program against Ann's authorizations. As a result, Paul, without bypassing the reference monitor, can access information he is not authorized to see by the stated access control policies.

Some of the drawbacks of DAC in terms of unauthorized information flow are overcome by Mandatory Access Control (MAC), whose early implementations mainly focused on the protection of military-oriented environments. According to MAC, authorizations are not explicitly specified. Rather, authorized accesses are derived from the security classification given to subjects and objects, on the basis of a set of rules that specify which relation should hold between a subject and object classification, because the first can gain access to the second. In the next sections, we first review the Bell and LaPadula model which represents the root of MAC. Then, in Sections 4.2 and 4.3, we

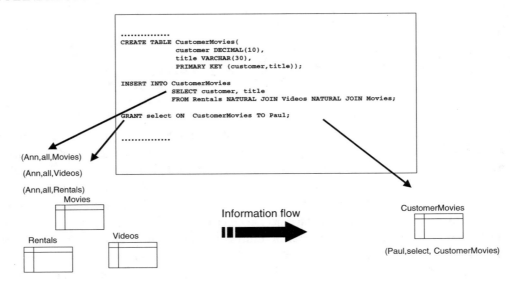

Figure 4.1: An example of Trojan Horse.

discuss how MAC can be applied to the relational and object data models, respectively. In Section 4.4, we discuss some of the hard problems to be solved in real-world MAC applications. Finally, in Section 4.5 we present some proposals aimed at combining DAC and MAC.

4.1 BELL AND LAPADULA MODEL

Many of the mandatory access control models proposed so far have been designed based on the Bell and LaPadula (BPL) model [Bell and LaPadula, 1975], specified for operating systems. In the BPL model subjects are either users or processes. The privileges supported by the model are: `read`, that allows a subject to read the information in an object; `append`, to modify an object; `write`, to both read and modify an object; and `execute`, to execute an object (e.g., an application program). In what follows, we consider only the `read`, `write`, and `append` privileges since they are those strictly related to data management. Additionally, for the sake of simplicity, some of the details of the model are omitted. In the BPL model, subjects and objects are assigned an *access class*. An access class consists of two components: a *security level* and a *set of categories*. The security level is an element from a totally ordered set, for instance: `Top Secret` (TS), `Secret` (S), `Confidential` (C), and `Unclassified` (U), where TS > S > C > U. The set of categories is a possibly empty set of elements, dependent from the application area in which the access control model is used. For instance, if we consider the military domain, examples of categories are: `Army`, `Navy`, `Air Force`, and `Nuclear`, whereas if we consider a commercial domain, examples of categories are: `Management`, `Sales`, and `R&D`. For instance, a file containing confidential management information can be assigned the following access class: (Confidential, {Management}), whereas an air marshal can be classified as (Top Secret,{Air Force,Nuclear}). Therefore, categories provide a fine grained classification of subjects and objects based on the domain they belong to, as such they are the basis to enforce the need to know principle (cfr. Chapter 1).

Because of their definition, access classes are a partially ordered set, defined by a *dominance* relationship $\geq$, formally defined as follows.

Definition 4.2   (Dominance relationship) An access class $ac_1 = (L_1, Cat_1)$ dominates an access class $ac_2 = (L_2, Cat_2)$, denoted as $ac_1 \geq ac_2$, if both of the following conditions hold: (i) the security level of ac_1 is greater than or equal to the security level of ac_2, that is, $L_1 \geq L_2$; (ii) the set of categories of ac_1 includes the set of categories of ac_2, that is, $Cat_1 \supseteq Cat_2$.

If $L_1 > L_2$ and $Cat_1 \supset Cat_2$, we say that ac_1 *strictly dominates* ac_2 (written $ac_1 > ac_2$). Finally, ac_1 and ac_2 are *incomparable* (written $ac_1 <> ac_2$), if neither $ac_1 \geq ac_2$ nor $ac_2 \geq ac_1$ hold.

Access classes and the dominance relationship defined as above form a lattice [Sandhu, 1993].

Example 4.3   Consider the following access classes:

ac_1 = (TS,{Nuclear,Navy})
ac_2 = (TS,{Nuclear})
ac_3 = (C,{Navy})

$ac_1 \geq ac_2$, since both ac_1 and ac_2 have the same security level, but the set of categories of ac_1 includes those of ac_2; $ac_1 > ac_3$, since TS > C and {Navy} is a proper subset of {Nuclear,Navy}. Finally, $ac_2 <> ac_3$; indeed, $ac_2 \not\geq ac_3$, since {Nuclear}$\not\supseteq$ {Navy} and $ac_3 \not\geq ac_2$, since TS > C.

The state of the system is described by the pair $(A, \mathcal{L})$[1], where:

- A is *the set of current accesses*, that is, the accesses currently under execution in the system; A is a set of triples (s, o, p), stating that subject s is exercising privilege p on object o.

- $\mathcal{L}$ is the *level function* that associates with each object and subject its access class. Formally, $\mathcal{L} : O \cup S \to \mathcal{AC}$, where O and S denote the set of objects and subjects in the system, respectively, and $\mathcal{AC}$ is the set of access classes.

Each update to the state of the system is performed through a *request*. Examples of requests are the request to access a given object, or the request to modify the access class of an object. The system answer is called *decision*. If a request is executed, this causes a transition of the system from one state to another (that is, the one resulting from the action required by the request). Given a

---

[1]In the original formulation of the BPL model, the state of the system is described by two more components, namely, the access matrix and the object hierarchy. For simplicity, we omit here these two components since they do not impact the following discussion.

request and the current state, the decision and the new state are determined on the basis of a set of axioms. These axioms define the conditions that should be satisfied to accept the request and therefore to perform a transition state. The system is *secure* if only the requests that verify the axioms are executed.

In what follows, we focus on access control requests. Access control requests are regulated by two axioms[2]:

Simple security property. A state $(A, \mathcal{L})$ satisfies the simple security property if, for each element $(s, o, p) \in A$ such that p=read or p=write: $\mathcal{L}(s) \geq \mathcal{L}(o)$.

The main goal of the simple security property is to prevent subjects from reading data with access classes dominating or incomparable with respect to their access class. It therefore ensures that subjects can read only information for which they have the necessary access class. The simple security property is also known as the *no read-up* property in that it avoids illegal flows of information originated by read operations on higher level objects.

Example 4.4   According to the simple security property, a subject with access class (C,{Navy}) is not allowed to read objects with access class: (C,{Navy,Air Force}) or (U,{Air Force}). In contrast, the subject can read objects with access class (U,{Navy}).

However, the simple security property is not enough to protect the system against any unauthorized flow of information, in particular those flows enacted by write operations. For instance, a subject with access class (TS, Ø) might read an object with access class (TS, Ø) and write the obtained information into an object with access class (U, Ø), without violating the simple security property. This would make Top Secret information available to Unclassified subjects. To avoid this, a further axiom has been added, specifically designed to regulate write operations.

$*$ **property** (read star property). A state $(A, \mathcal{L})$ satisfies the $*$ property if, for each element $(s, o, p) \in A$ such that p=append or p=write: $\mathcal{L}(s) \leq \mathcal{L}(o)$.

The $*$ property, known also as the *no write-down* property, has been designed to prevent unauthorized flows of information due to write operations on lower or incomparable objects.

Example 4.5   According to the $*$ property, a subject with access class (C,{Army,Nuclear}) is not allowed to write on objects with access class (U,{Army,Nuclear}), since these objects are accessible to subjects that, according to their classification, are not allowed to read information classified as (C,{Army,Nuclear}).

However, the applications of the two properties above may result in too rigid restrictions that may prevent common activities in the system, as the following example shows.

Example 4.6   Consider once again the military domain and suppose that (TS,{Army, Nuclear}) is the access class associated with a general, say Matt, whereas one of his colonels has access class

---

[2]In what follows, the terms axiom and property are used synonymously.

(C,{Army}). According to the BPL axioms, the colonel can communicate with the general, since he can exercise the append privilege on objects with higher access classes. In contrast, Matt cannot communicate with his/her colonel since the ∗ property prevents write operations on lower level objects.

To avoid situations like the one discussed in Example 4.6, users can connect to the system at any access class lower then the one assigned to them. When a user connects to the system with a certain access class, he/she is considered by the system as a subject with an access class equal to the one the user has selected to connect to the system. So, for instance, to be able to communicate with his colonel, the general in Example 4.6 can connect to the system with access class (C,{Army}).

As far as access control is concerned, a system is *secure* if, for each element added to the set of current accesses, both the simple security and the ∗ property are satisfied.

Example 4.7   Consider Example 4.1 and let us see how the Trojan Horse can be avoided by the BPL model. For simplicity, we consider access classes consisting only of the security level component. A possible classification that reflects the sensitivity of the managed information and the clearance of the involved users is as follows: Secret for Ann and relation Rentals, storing information on the movies rented by the customers of the video library, and Unclassified for Paul and relation CustomerMovies. When Ann runs the application she receives from Paul, the authorized accesses depend on the access class she chooses for the connection. If she connects at the Confidential/Secret level, the write operation on CustomerMovies is prevented by the ∗ property, whereas if she connects at the Unclassified level the read operation on Rentals is prevented, because of the simple security property. In both cases, the unauthorized transfer of information to Paul described in Example 4.1 does not take place.

A side effect of the ∗ property is that an Unclassified user may append information into a Secret file and this may cause integrity problems. To avoid this situation, when BPL axioms are applied to DMSs, write up operations are usually prevented. This means that subjects can only modify objects who have access class the same as the one of the subject.

It is important to note that the definition of secure system given above does not totally guarantee the security of the system, as shown by McLean [1990]. For instance, consider a system with the following access control policy: whenever a subject s requests any type of access on an object o, the access class of each object/subject is set to the lowest one and the access is granted. A system enforcing this policy satisfies the BLP definition of secure system. However, it is obviously not secure in that after the first access, everybody can access everything. The reason for this is that the BLP model offers strong security guarantees only when subject and object access classes do not change during normal operation of the system (this property is also known as *strong tranquility principle*). If this principle is not enforced, the security of the system depends on how the access classes of subjects and objects can be modified. However, the strong tranquility principle is too strict to be widely applied in real world scenarios, since it requires that subjects and objects are statically assigned to their access classes. Indeed, it may often be the case that subjects and objects should be dynamically assigned to different access classes on the basis of the system evolution. For this purpose, alternative less restrictive principles have been defined that allow the modification of access classes under specific conditions. Moreover, to allow for more flexibility, the notion of *trusted subject* is introduced, as a subject to which some of the restrictions of MAC does not apply. This, for instance, is supported by Oracle Label Security [Oracle Corporation, 2009], the component of Oracle DMS providing mandatory access control.

4.2   MULTILEVEL RELATIONAL DATA MODEL

The original formulation of the BPL model has been designed for protecting objects in an operating system environment. In such an environment, objects are mainly files. The first issue to be dealt with when applying MAC to DMSs is that objects to be protected are at a variety of granularity levels. If we consider the relational data model, an object can be a whole relation, but also a selected tuple within a relation, an attribute, or the value of an attribute for a specific tuple (data element). This means that an access class can be in principle assigned to all these objects. For instance, if we consider the `Rentals` relation of our running example, the rental of different movies may have different sensitivity levels and this may result in different access classes assigned to the tuples of the `Rentals` relation, or to selected attributes of a tuple (e.g., the title of the movie).

A *multilevel relational DMS* should therefore represent multiple versions of the same entity, action, or event at different security levels[3], without violating the integrity of the database or the access control rules. The finer the granularity of security levels, the more difficult it is to achieve this goal. Addressing this issue requires extensions to the relational model itself and to some of its basic concepts, such as, for instance, the notion of primary key. This has been achieved by defining the so-called *multilevel relational data model*, characterized by the fact that each attribute of a relation has an associated security level.

The key mechanism to represent multiple versions of an entity at different security levels is called *polyinstantiation*, a term firstly used in the framework of the SeaView project [Lunt et al., 1990]. Polyinstantiation enables two tuples with the same primary key to exist in a relational database at different security levels. However, having two tuples with the same primary key violates the integrity property of the standard relational data model. In contrast, if polyinstantiation is not supported, then it is possible for signaling channels to occur.

To understand the problem, let us consider the `Emp` multilevel relation in Figure 4.2, where a security level is attached to each data element, and attribute `name` is the key. For simplicity, we consider only two security levels: U (Unclassified) and S (Secret). Different subjects have different views of the relation in Figure 4.2, depending on their security classification. For instance, Figure 4.3 reports the view of the relation in Figure 4.2 for an Unclassified subject.

The first obvious constraint that should hold to not violate the integrity constraints implied by primary keys is that: *1)* all the attributes forming a primary key should have the same classification;

---

[3]In what follows, for simplicity, we consider access classes consisting only of security levels.

name	L	age	L	salary	L
Leo	U	28	U	50K	U
Ann	U	35	S	100K	U
Marc	S	40	S	95K	S

Figure 4.2:   An example of multilevel relation.

name	L	age	L	salary	L
Leo	U	28	U	50K	U
Ann	U	-	U	100K	U

Figure 4.3:   The view of Emp for Unclassified subjects.

name	L	age	L	salary	L
Leo	U	28	U	50K	U
Ann	U	35	S	100K	U
Marc	S	40	S	95K	S
Marc	U	40	U	100K	U

Figure 4.4:   An example of polyinstantiated relation.

and *2)* the classification of non-key attributes should dominate the one of key attributes, otherwise the view at some level may contain a null value for key attributes.

Now suppose that an Unclassified subject requests the insertion of the tuple (Marc,40,100) into the Emp relation of Figure 4.2. If the tuple is accepted, then it violates the primary key constraint, since a tuple already exists in the relation whose attribute name is equal to Marc. In contrast, if the tuple is rejected due to an integrity violation, then the actions of a Secret subject have interfered with those of an Unclassified one, and this causes a secrecy violation since the Unclassified subject would know the existence of an higher tuple referring to Marc. Finally, if the Unclassified tuple overwrites the Secret one, this is in principle acceptable from a pure security point of view. However, this solution may not be acceptable in many cases since Secret data would be lost. Polyinstantiation allows the simultaneous presence of the two tuples, the resulting relation is shown in Figure 4.4.

A similar problem arises for update operations requested by Unclassified subjects. For instance, with reference to Figure 4.2, an Unclassified subject may request to update Ann's age. Refusing the update operation compromises secrecy, whereas overriding the Secret value would compromise integrity. With *attribute polyinstantiation*, two tuples may exist for Ann, with two different values for attribute Age, with Secret and Unclassified level, respectively. Polystantiation may also be caused by insertion/update operations performed by Secret subjects. For instance, consider again the Emp relation of Figure 4.2, and suppose that a Secret subject requires the insertion of the tuple (Leo,29,100).

Overriding the existing tuple causes a covert channel, whereas denying the insertion would cause a Denial-of-Service for the Secret user. Polyinstantiation allows the simultaneous presence of two tuples referring to Leo, with different security levels.

Earlier work on multilevel relational DMSs consider polyinstantiation necessary to design multilevel database systems with higher levels of assurance (see, for example, Denning et al. [1987]). Some argue that it is important to maintain the integrity of the data and that polyinstantiation violates the integrity (see, for example, Burns [1990]). Some have used partial polyinstantiation together with security constraint enforcement (see, for example, Sandhu and Chen [1998]; Stachour and Thuraisingham [1990]) to preserve data integrity in the presence of polyinstantiation. Others have attempted to give a precise semantics of the database states in the presence of polyinstantiation. However, probably because of all the side-effects connected with polyinstantiation, fine-grained multilevel relational DMSs did not have much success, and DMSs supporting MAC restrict the granularity of access classes at the tuple level.

Differently from DAC, MAC is not directly supported by SQL. However, since 1988, Multi-level Secure relational DMS products have been developed (e.g., Sybase's Secure SQL Server, Trusted Oracle, Trusted Informix) but some of these products are not on the market anymore because of the lack of success that confined them into a market niche. Furthermore, some of the corporations have merged so the ownership of these products has also changed. However, recently, there is a renewed interest in the basic principles underlying MAC [Saydjari, 2004], because of the strong security guarantees required today by many non-military applications. This has resulted in a revitalization of the market, see, for instance, Oracle Label Security [Oracle Corporation, 2009], or implementations such as SELinux (incorporated into Linux kernels since version 2.6) and Mandatory Integrity Control (incorporated into Windows Vista and newer).

4.3   MANDATORY ACCESS CONTROL FOR OBJECT DMSS

The application of MAC to the object data model requires addressing a number of issues due to the semantic richness of the object model and the fact that objects consist of both attributes and methods. Additionally, the task is further complicated by the lack of a well-accepted standard for both the object data model and the related query language [Olivier and von Solms, 1994]. Up until now the research has focused on object-oriented DMSs only, whereas we are not aware of any proposal for the object-relational data model.

Keefe et al. [1989] were the first to incorporate multilevel security in the object-oriented data model. The resulting model is called SODA (Secure Object-oriented DAtabase). In SODA, both objects or instance variables are assigned ranges of sensitivity levels, whereas subjects are assigned clearance levels. A method activation is assigned a current classification level and a clearance level, that is the same as that of the associated user and serves as an upper bound on the current classification level. Authorized operations are designed to enforce the BPL properties. For this purpose, a set of rules determines whether a method should be permitted access to an object or variable, on the basis of the method current sensitivity and clearance level, and the object's or variable's sensitivity level.

Method activations in SODA have their classifications dynamically upgraded whenever an object or variable with a higher sensitivity is accessed. More details can be found in Keefe et al. [1989].

Thuraisingham also investigated MAC in the framework of the ORION object-oriented data model. The resulting model was called SORION [Thuraisingham, 1989]. In SORION, subjects and objects are assigned security levels. Protection objects include classes, their instances, methods, and instance variables. SORION defines a set of constraints that the protection object security levels must satisfy. For instance, the security levels of the instances of a class must dominate the security level of the class, whereas the security level of a subclass must dominate the security level of the superclass. Other constraints are defined on the security levels of methods, for instance the one that implies that the security level of a method must be greater than the least upper bound of the security levels of the classes in its domain. SORION enforces the BPL axioms stated in Section 4.1. Other rules have been added to deal with method execution. More precisely, in SORION, a subject can execute a method if the subject's security level dominates the security level of the method and that of the class with which the method is associated. A method executes at the level of the subject who initiated the execution; during the execution of a method m_1, if another method m_2 has to be executed, then m_2 can execute only if the execution level of m_1 dominates the level of m_2 and of the class with which m_2 is associated. Reading and writing of objects during method execution are governed by the BPL axioms.

A different approach has been introduced by Jajodia and Kogan [1990], who proposed enforcing MAC on the basis of a message-filtering algorithm. According to this model, objects can communicate only by means of messages. Every message is intercepted by the message filter that determines, on the basis of the message type and the classifications of the sender and receiver, if the message will cause an illegal flow of information within the system. All more complex messages are divided into a sequence of messages of the following four types: 1) read: a method that reads the value of an attribute; 2) write: a method that modifies the value of an attribute; 3) invoke: a method that invokes another method via the sending of a message; and 4) create: a method that creates a new object. Different filtering rules are enforced depending on whether the messages are sent from one object to another, or from an object to itself (for instance, for object creation).

4.4 MAC VS DAC

Although mandatory policies provide stronger security guarantees than DAC, they are still vulnerable to security threats originated by *covert channels*. A covert channel allows the transfer of information that violates the security policy. Covert channels are usually classified into two broad categories: *storage* and *timing* channels, depending on what is exploited to transfer the information. In timing channels the information is conveyed by the timings of events or processes, whereas storage channels do not require any temporal synchronization since they exploit access to system information. Therefore, the development of a MLS/DMS requires not only the extension of the underlying data model, but also the main components of the system architecture in order to close all the possible covert channels [U.S. Department of Defense, 1975]. For instance, a well-known covert channel in multilevel DMSs is based on the exploitation of the two Phase Locking (2PL) concurrency control protocol, as the following example shows.

Example 4.8   Consider a multilevel relational database storing information at two different security levels: Unclassified (U) and Confidential (C), and suppose that accesses are governed by the BPL axioms. Consider two transactions T_U and T_C with security level Unclassified and Confidential, respectively, and an Unclassified data item d_1. Suppose now that T_C requires a read lock on d_1. The lock is granted, because no other transaction has a lock on d_1. Suppose now that transaction T_U wishes to write d_1. Therefore, it requires a write lock on d_1. Since transaction T_C holds a read lock on d_1, transaction T_U has to wait until T_C releases its lock. By selectively issuing requests to read Unclassified data, transaction T_C can modulate the delay experienced by transaction T_U. Since, T_C has full access to classified data, this delay can be used to transfer confidential information to transaction T_U. Thus, a timing channel is established between the two transactions.

Moreover, other forms of covert channels can be established if system resources and/or system information are not properly managed and protected. This happens, for instance, when an Unclassified subject can access information on the resource usage made by Confidential subjects, or when information on data locks are visible to Unclassified subjects.

The above examples have been provided only to demonstrate that MAC does not fully protect against attacks through covert channels and therefore needs to be engineered in order to close all covert channels. For instance, with reference to concurrency control, many alternative protocols have been proposed. The majority of such proposals are based on the principle that transactions cannot be delayed or aborted, because of a lock conflict with a higher level transaction. Therefore, low-level transactions always have higher priority on low-level data than higher-level transactions. The consequence is that even though a transaction may have acquired a read lock on a lower-level data item, it may be forced to release this lock if a lower-level transaction requires a write lock on it. Because of such priority, transaction execution histories may not be always serializable. Several approaches have been proposed to address the issue of how to synchronize transactions so that timing channels do not occur and at the same time serializability is achieved. However, they suffer from several shortcomings, such as starvation of high-level transactions, that can be repeatedly aborted, or they require multiple versions of data, or force high-level transactions to read stale data. To overcome these limitations, Bertino et al. [2001c] proposed an approach based on the use of nested transactions and single-version data items. The developed concurrency control mechanism, based on application-level recovery and notification-based locking protocols, it is free of timing channels and avoids many of the shortcomings of the previously developed concurrency control mechanisms, such as transaction starvation and resource waste. However, although the problem of designing concurrency control algorithms free of timing channels has been extensively investigated, most of the research proposals have not been engineered into any commercial DMSs. The only exception is represented by Trusted Oracle whose concurrency control mechanism was based on 2PL combined with multiversion techniques in order to avoid timing channels. However, such algorithm does not generate serializable schedules [Atluri et al., 1996].

Another notable hard problem is the inference problem. Inference happens when, by posing queries, a subject is able to deduce sensitive information from the legitimate responses received. Many efforts have been discussed in literature to handle the inference problem. Thuraisingham [1991] proved that the general inference problem was unsolvable. This means that a complete and general solution to the inference problem is impossible. Therefore, most of the work done so far provides solution only for particular types of inferences [Farkas and Jajodia, 2002]. The definition of a practical solution that offers reasonable security guarantees is still an open issue.

4.5   INFORMATION-FLOW CONTROL MODELS

An alternative way to overcome the drawbacks of MAC and DAC is to complement discretionary access control with some form of flow control, borrowing some ideas from MAC. Along this line is, for instance, the approach by Karger [1987] that restricts programs to access objects satisfying given patterns only. Other approaches (e.g., McCollum et al. [1990]) prevent unauthorized information flow by propagating the access control list associated with an object, once its information has been accessed. The work by Samarati et al. [1997] enforces information flow control by means of the so-called *strict* policy, based on the same principles as the mandatory policy. According to the strict policy, a process can write an object o only if o is at least as *read-protected* as all the objects read by the process up to that point. An object o is at least as read-protected as another object o' if the set of subjects allowed to read o is contained in the set of subjects allowed to read o'. The model is still discretionary in that authorizations are explicitly specified, however the strict policy reduces the flexibility of the system. Indeed, after reading an object o, a process is unable to write any object less read-protected than o, even if this write operation would not result in any improper information leakage.

Bertino et al. [1998b] presented a flow control model for object-oriented systems that allows for more flexibility in the enforcement of the strict policy. The model is based on the observation that blocking or allowing a write operation required by a process ultimately depends on the information such an operation releases, and not on the information accessed by the process. A process may access sensitive data, and yet not release any sensitive information through the write operations it executes. Such write operations should therefore be allowed. Alternatively, information released by a process may be more sensitive than the information that the process has accessed. Although they do not violate the strict policy, write operations releasing this sensitive information should be blocked. These situations may be handled through *exceptions* (either more restrictive or permissive) to the strict policy. As an example of the benefits of these exceptions, consider a procedure accessing personal information regarding employees of an organization and returning the benefits to be granted to each employee. The benefits of each employee can be released to users not authorized to read the information provided as input of the benefit calculation (e.g., salaries, evaluations).

Therefore, each procedure may have associated a set of exceptions to the restrictions/permissions stated by discretionary authorizations. Exceptions can be of two different types: invoke exceptions, applicable within a method execution, and reply exceptions, applicable to the information returned by a method. Exceptions can be permissive (that is, they override a restriction imposed by the strict policy) or restrictive (that is, they override a permission stated by the strict policy). The enforcement mechanism is based on the notion of message filter, first introduced by Jajodia and Kogan [1990] (cfr. Section 4.3). To determine whether a write operation should be blocked, the message filter proposed by Bertino et al. [1998b] keeps track of the information transmitted between method executions together with the users to whom the information can be released. A write operation on object o is authorized by the message filter if, based on the authorizations on the objects read and on the exceptions encountered, the information can be released to all users who have read privileges on o.

A more recent work is the FlexFlow logic based framework proposed by Chen et al. [2003], where a variety of control flow policies may be specified as a set of stratified Horn clauses. The framework has been further extended by Alghathbar et al. [2006] to specify and validate information flow policies in UML-based designs.

CHAPTER 5

Role-based Access Control

One challenging problem in managing large systems is the complexity of security administration. Security administration entails, among other tasks, assigning and revoking authorizations to subjects on the objects to be protected. Whenever the number of subjects and objects is high, the number of such authorizations can become extremely large. If, moreover, the user population is highly dynamic, the number of grant and revoke operations to be performed can become very difficult to manage. Role-based Access Control (RBAC) has been proposed as an alternative approach to traditional discretionary and mandatory access control with the goal of simplifying authorization administration [Ferraiolo et al., 2001].

The basic idea underlying RBAC is based on the simple consideration that the permissions a user has on the data he/she manages are generally related to his/her functions within an organization, rather than on his/her identity. Therefore, the key component of RBAC is the concept of *role* – a function within a given organization to which a set of privileges are assigned. The privileges assigned to a role are related to the authorizations needed to perform the corresponding job function. Access authorizations are then granted to roles instead of to single users. Users are then simply authorized to "play" the appropriate roles, thereby acquiring the roles' authorizations. This means that between objects and subjects a further level is introduced, that is, the level of roles, with the aim of simplifying authorization administration. A milestone of RBAC is the paper by Sandhu et al. [1996], that defined a family of RBAC models, known as the RBAC96 model.

The use of roles has several, well-recognized advantages. First of all, because roles represent organizational functions, an RBAC model makes the mapping of organization access control policies onto a set of authorizations easier. Authorization administration is also greatly simplified. First of all, the number of roles is usually much fewer than the number of users. Moreover, because of their semantics, roles are far more stable than users that can frequently change their function within the system. For instance, if a user moves to a new function within the organization, this does not have any impact on the roles and their authorizations. Therefore, there is no need, as in traditional discretionary access control models, to revoke the authorizations he/she had in the previous function and grant the authorizations he/she needs in the new function. The security administrator simply needs to revoke and grant the appropriate role membership. Finally, RBAC has been shown to be policy-neutral [Osborn et al., 2000] since, by appropriately configuring the set of roles, one can support different policies, including the mandatory and discretionary ones.

Because of its relevance, RBAC has been widely investigated, resulting in several role-based access control models for a variety of application domains [Zhang and Joshi, 2009]. RBAC has also attracted the attention of the main DMS vendors (e.g., Oracle, DB2, Microsoft SQL Server,

PostgreSQL), who have incorporated the support for roles in their products. These different implementations have created a standardization problem, since often the same term has been used with different meanings by the various models, or the same concept has different interpretations. To overcome this problem, a standardization effort, both in terminology and classification of models, has been undertaken, which has resulted first in the NIST RBAC standard [Ferraiolo et al., 2001] which was later modified in 2004 into the ANSI/INCITS standard [ANSI, 2004]. In what follows, we first illustrate the ANSI/INCITS RBAC standard and the support to RBAC provided by SQL. Then, in Section 5.3 we address the problem of role administration. Finally, we conclude the chapter by discussing of the main extensions to RBAC96 and the NIST standard proposed so far.

5.1   THE ANSI/INCITS RBAC STANDARD

The ANSI/INCITS RBAC standard [ANSI, 2004] has been modularly conceived so that it can be customized for different needs and environments. It consists of three components: *Core RBAC*, *Hierarchical RBAC*, and *Constrained RBAC*. Core RBAC standardizes the basic features that any RBAC model should posses, whereas *Hierarchical RBAC* and *Constrained RBAC* are two independent extensions of Core RBAC. Hierarchical RBAC adds to Core RBAC the support for role hierarchies, whereas Constrained RBAC adds to Core RBAC the support for separation of duties constraints. By combining these modules, RBAC can adapt to different environments and application domains. In what follows, we illustrate the three main components of the standard in more details.

5.1.1   CORE RBAC

Core RBAC is a model consisting of the following four components: a set of users *USERS*, a set of roles *ROLES*, a set of permissions *PRMS*, and a set of sessions *SESSIONS*.

A *user* is essentially a human being, although the concept of user may be extended to include a machine, a network, a process, or an intelligent autonomous agent. A *role* is a function within the context of an organization with an associated semantics regarding its authority and responsibility. A *permission* is the right to perform a certain action on a given object in the system. More precisely, *PRMS* is a set of pairs (obj, op), where $obj \in OBS$ is an object from the set of protected objects *OBS*, and $op \in OPS$ denotes an operation from the set OPS of operations allowed in the system. Clearly, the members of OBS and OPS depend on the system being protected.

Sessions have been introduced to model the fact that, when a user logs in the system, he/she may activate a subset of the roles he/she is authorized to play. Therefore, a session maps a given user to the set of active roles and determines the set of permissions the user holds during the session.

Besides defining the core components, Core RBAC also defines the relationships that exist among them, the most relevant ones are illustrated in Table 5.1. With reference to Table 5.1, UA and PA identify many-to-many relations, in that a user may be assigned to many roles (all the ones needed to perform his/her functions within a given organization), and a role may be assigned to different users (that is, all the users authorized to take the associated job function). Similarly, a permission may be assigned to many roles (all the roles that need this permission to perform the

Table 5.1: Mappings defined for Core RBAC

Mapping	Meaning
$UA \subseteq USERS \times ROLES$	user-role assignment, it specifies the roles users are enabled to play
$PA \subseteq PRMS \times ROLES$	permission-role assignment, it assigns roles the permissions needed to complete their jobs
$Assigned\_prms: ROLES \to 2^{PRMS}$	it maps a role onto the set of assigned permissions, $Assigned\_prms(r) = \{p \mid p \in PRMS, (p, r) \in PA\}$
$Assigned\_users: ROLES \to 2^{USERS}$	it maps a role onto the set of associated users, $Assigned\_users(r) = \{u \mid u \in USERS, (u, r) \in UA\}$
$Session\_usr: SESSIONS \to USERS$	it maps a session onto the corresponding user
$Session\_roles: SESSIONS \to 2^{ROLES}$	it maps a session onto a set of roles, $Session\_roles(s) \subseteq \{r \in ROLES \mid (Session\_usr(s), r) \in UA\}$
$Avl\_sess\_prms: SESSIONS \to 2^{PRMS}$	it gives the set of permissions available to a user during a session, $Avl\_sess\_prms(s) = \bigcup_{r \in Session\_roles(s)} Assigned\_prms(r)$

corresponding job function), and a role may be given many permissions (all the ones needed to perform the corresponding function). A user may activate many sessions, but each session refers to a single user. A session may be associated with many roles (all the roles that are activated by the user to which the session belongs to), and the same role may be associated with different sessions (all the sessions where it has been activated). Clearly, the constraint exists that the set of roles activated during a session s be a subset of the roles assigned to the user u establishing the session, whereas the permissions u can exercise in the section are given by the union of the set of permissions associated with the roles activated by u in s.

Example 5.1   A typical domain of application for RBAC is the healthcare environment. In such an environment typical functions that can be modeled as roles include nurse, patient, doctor, voluntary personnel, and researcher, whereas examples of data to be protected include patients' name, address, clinical data, and anonymized statistical data. Once roles have been defined and permissions have been associated with them, users may be assigned to roles. For example, when a new person joins the healthcare staff, the only required management action is to authorize him/her to play the appropriate roles, instead of granting him/her all the necessary permissions individually. Similarly, when a user leaves the healthcare staff, this simply requires revoking from the user the authorization to play the roles corresponding to his/her functions as staff (these are usually significantly less than the number of access permissions the user was authorized to exercise).

5.1.2   HIERARCHICAL RBAC

Core RBAC, also known as flat RBAC, does not support any structuring of the set of roles. However, it is often the case that roles are hierarchically structured within an organization to reflect a line of authority and responsibility. Such a requirement is captured by Hierarchical RBAC, which adds to Core RBAC the possibility of structuring roles into an hierarchy. For this purpose, a partial order relation on $ROLES$ is introduced, referred to as *role hierarchy*. The role hierarchy, defined as $RH \subseteq ROLES \times ROLES$, and denoted as $\geq$, identifies the pairs of roles (r_i, r_j) such that role r_i inherits from role r_j. The role hierarchy implies a relation among *a)* the permissions associated with the roles in the hierarchy and *b)* the set of users authorized to play the roles in the hierarchy. More precisely, given two roles $r_1, r_2 \in ROLES, r_1 \geq r_2$[1] implies that:

1. r_1 inherits all the permissions associated with r_2, that is, $Assigned\_prms(r_2) \subseteq Assigned\_prms(r_1)$;

2. All users associated with r_1 are also users associated with r_2, that is, $Assigned\_users(r_1) \subseteq Assigned\_users(r_2)$.

The principles above are motivated by the fact that usually a role should be authorized to perform on the objects in the system all the operations that are allowed to its junior roles. Clearly, there could be situations where this general principle does not work. For instance, consider a critical infrastructure where only some highly skilled employees are able to perform certain operations, whereas their supervisors are not. This exception can be handled by configuring the role hierarchy in such a way that the roles corresponding to the highly skilled employees and their supervisors are not linked by the inheritance relation.

Therefore, in the presence of a role hierarchy, the definition of *Assigned_prms* and *Assigned_users* (cfr. Table 5.1) is modified in such a way that they make a transitive closure of the non hierarchical mappings with respect to the role hierarchy, that is, given $r, r' \in ROLES$:

- $Assigned\_prms_H(r) = Assigned\_prms(r) \cup \{p \mid p \in Assigned\_prms(r'), r \geq r'\}$;

- $Assigned\_users_H(r) = Assigned\_users(r) \cup \{u \mid u \in Assigned\_users(r'), r' \geq r\}$.

In general, role inheritance represents an additional means to reduce the burden of authorization management. For instance, when a new kind of data is made available to the system, what is needed is only to identify, in the role hierarchy, the least privileged roles that must be able to access it, and grant the appropriate permissions to them, thus greatly reducing the number of needed grant operations.

Example 5.2   An example of role hierarchy referring to the healthcare domain is depicted in Figure 5.1. According to Figure 5.1, users assigned to roles Cardiologist, Dermatologist, Specialist,

---

[1] r_1 is the *senior role*, whereas r_2 is the *junior role*.

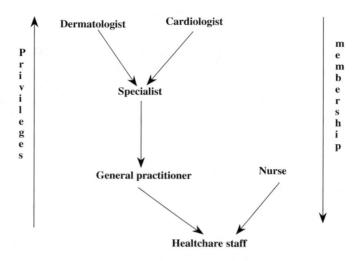

Figure 5.1: An example of role hierarchy.

General practitioner and Nurse are all members of the role Healthcare staff. A dermatologist has all the authorizations given to a general practitioner. Moreover, he/she can have additional authorizations with respect to the ones given to general practitioners.

The definition of role hierarchy given so far (referred to as *general role hierarchy*), does not impose any restriction to the partial order that serves as the role hierarchy, which may include the concept of multiple inheritance, that is, a role may inherit from many roles. However, many data management systems impose restrictions on the role hierarchy, the most common one is that hierarchies are limited to simple structures such as trees or inverted trees. The support for this concept is achieved in the standard by introducing the notion of *limited role hierarchy*.

5.1.3   CONSTRAINED RBAC

Constrained RBAC adds to Core RBAC the possibility of expressing constraints on roles and their assignment to users. In its current form, the standard provides support for one type of constraint only, that is, *Separation of Duties (SoD) constraints*. SoD is the most investigated type of constraint, because of its relevance in many application domains. Other relevant classes of constraints, such as cardinality constraints [Ferraiolo et al., 1999] or temporal constraints [Bertino et al., 2001a; Joshi et al., 2005] are not yet considered by the standard.

SoD is a widely studied and relevant concept that aims at reducing the risk of fraud by not allowing any individual to have sufficient authority within the system to perpetuate a fraud on his/her own. This can be achieved in two different ways that result in two different classes of SoD constraints supported by the standard, that is, *static* and *dynamic* SoD.

Static SoD constraints define a mutual exclusion (or conflict of interests) relation among the roles a user is authorized to play. For instance, there may exist an organizational policy stating that if a user is authorized to play the role of town clerk, he/she cannot be authorized to play the role of auditor, since the second role has the duty of controlling the operations made by the first. In the standard, the notion of non-compatible roles is generalized to more than two roles, in order to support a variety of different SoD requirements. More formally, a static SoD constraint is a pair (RS, n), where $RS \subseteq ROLES$, and n is a natural number greater than one. The constraint (RS, n) states that a user can be authorized to play no more than $n - 1$ roles among those in RS. If roles are hierarchically structured such constraint propagates along the role hierarchy in that both inherited and directly assigned roles are considered when enforcing the constraint.

The second option is referred to as *dynamic SoD*, in that the constraint must be dynamically validated, by guaranteeing at the time of role activation that a user is prevented from activating conflicting roles within the same session. This differs from static SoD constraints that can be statically checked at the time of role assignment. Similar to static SoD constraints, dynamic SoD constraints are also represented as pairs (RS, n), where $RS \subseteq ROLES$, and n is a natural number greater than one. However, the semantics is different in that a dynamic SoD constraint (RS, n) states that a user may not activate n or more roles from RS within a single session. Both forms of mutual exclusion constraints are relevant for several application environments, as the following example shows.

Example 5.3   Consider once again the healthcare domain. In such an environment, it is possible to identify several cases requiring both kinds of separation of duties. An example of static separation of duties is the intuitive prohibition to play both the nurse and doctor role, whereas an example of dynamic separation of duties is that a doctor cannot have himself/herself as a patient. Such constraint can be enforced by requiring that the roles doctor and patient cannot be activated by a user within the same session, whereas the same user can play the roles of doctor and patient in different sessions.

Figure 5.2 gives a graphical representation of the three components of the standard. Arrows indicate the cardinality of the relations (i.e., many-to-many, one-to-many).

A detailed critical analysis of the RBAC standard has been done by Li et al. [2007] where a set of critical issues have been identified and suggestions have been made on how they can be addressed. Among the criticality identified by Li et al. [2007] are the fact that the standard does not accommodate the design that only one role can be activated in a session. This solution, which is adopted by some RBAC systems (e.g., SELinux), provides better support of the least privilege principle (cfr. Chapter 1). Other critical issues identified are related to the role hierarchy. In particular, they argue that the use of partial orders to represent role hierarchies may be inappropriate when updates to the role hierarchy are considered. Furthermore, a better specification of the semantics of role inheritance is needed in that the standard leaves open several possible interpretations of a role hierarchy (e.g., user inheritance, permission inheritance). An answer to these concerns is discussed by Ferraiolo et al. [2007].

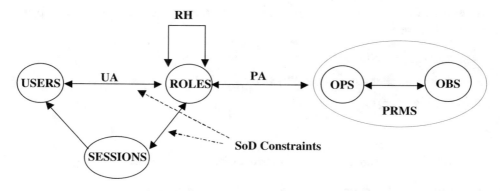

Figure 5.2: ANSI/INCITS RBAC standard.

5.2   RBAC SUPPORT IN SQL

DMS vendors have recognized the importance and the advantages of RBAC, and today most of commercial DMSs offer RBAC features at some extents. This interest has also been reflected in the current version of the SQL standard [ISO, 2003] that provides support for RBAC. In the following, we briefly presents the SQL commands related to role management.

   Roles can be created through the command CREATE ROLE ⟨role_name⟩, and deleted with the command DROP ROLE ⟨role_name⟩, where role_name denotes the name of the role to be created/deleted, respectively.

   Once a role has been created, privileges can be assigned to it through the GRANT command, whose basic format for what concerns privileges assignment to roles, has the following syntax:

```
GRANT {<privileges> | ALL PRIVILEGES}
ON [<object_type>] <object_name>
TO {<roles> | PUBLIC};
```

where:

- <privileges> denotes the set of operations authorized with the GRANT command. The keyword ALL PRIVILEGES denotes the set of all the supported operations.

- <object_name> is the object on which the authorization is granted. In some cases, it is necessary to specify what the type is of the object to be protected (for instance, TYPE is used for user-defined types).

- <roles> denotes the set of roles to which the privileges are granted. Keyword PUBLIC is used to denote all the roles in the system.

Moreover, the GRANT command can also be used to assign users/roles to roles. In this case, the syntax is as follows:

```
GRANT <granted_roles>
TO {<users> | <roles> | PUBLIC}
[WITH ADMIN OPTION];
```

where:

- <granted_roles> is the set of roles granted with the command.

- <users>/<roles> denotes the list of users/roles authorized to play the roles granted by the command. The keyword PUBLIC is used to authorize all the users/roles in the system to play the roles granted by the command.

- If the optional clause WITH ADMIN OPTION is specified, this means that who is authorized to play the specified roles can not only exercise all the privileges assigned to the roles but also grant others the authorization to play the specified roles. It is therefore similar to the grant option illustrated in Section 2.2 but it applies to roles instead of to privileges.

It is important to note that, according to the syntax of the GRANT command, it is possible to authorize a role to play another role. This is the way according to which the SQL standard supports role hierarchies, whereas in its current version it does not provide any support for SoD constraints.

Example 5.4   Consider once again Example 5.1 and Figure 5.1. The following are examples of commands related to role management:

```
CREATE ROLE Nurse;
CREATE ROLE Cardiologist;
CREATE ROLE Healthcare_staff;
GRANT select(name,address) ON Patients TO Healthcare_staff;
GRANT Nurse TO John WITH ADMIN OPTION;
GRANT Cardiologist TO Ann;
GRANT Healthcare_staff TO Nurse;
```

The first three commands create roles Nurse, Cardiologist, and Healthcare_staff, respectively, whereas the fourth command authorizes the role Healthcare_staff to query the name and address of patients. By the fifth command, John is authorized to play the role Nurse as well as to grant others the authorization to play that role, whereas by the sixth command Ann is authorized to play the role Cardiologist but not to grant others the authorization to play this role. Finally, the last command establishes a hierarchical relation between the roles Healthcare_staff and Nurse, that is, Nurse $\geq$ Healthcare_Staff (cfr. Section 5.1.2). One effect of this command is that John is authorized to query the name and address attributes of the Patients relation.

Roles can be activated within a session through the command SET ROLE.
Finally, privileges can be revoked from roles through the REVOKE command, whose syntax is as follows:

```
REVOKE <privileges>
ON [<object_type>] <object_name>
FROM <roles>
{RESTRICT|CASCADE};
```

where:

- <privileges> denotes the set of privileges being revoked;

- <object_name> is the object on which the privileges are revoked. In some cases, it is necessary to also specify what the type is of the object on which privileges are revoked;

- <roles> denotes the set of roles from which the privileges are revoked;

- RESTRICT and CASCADE are used to manage the side effects of the revoke operation, with the same meaning explained in Section 2.2.5. The default is RESTRICT.

The REVOKE command can also be used to revoke the authorization to play a role. In this case, the syntax is as follows:

```
REVOKE [ADMIN OPTION FOR] <revoked_roles>
FROM {<users> | <roles>}
{RESTRICT | CASCADE};
```

where:

- If the optional clause ADMIN OPTION FOR is specified, the effect of the command is to revoke the admin option only, still maintaining the authorization to play the roles listed in the REVOKE command.

- <revoked_roles> denotes the set of roles being revoked.

- <users>/<roles> denotes the set of users/roles to which the authorization to play the roles is being revoked.

- RESTRICT and CASCADE have the same meaning explained in Section 2.2.5.

Example 5.5   Consider the GRANT commands of Example 5.4. The following are examples of REVOKE commands:

```
REVOKE ADMIN OPTION FOR Nurse FROM John;

REVOKE select ON Patients FROM Healthcare_staff;

REVOKE Cardiologist FROM Ann;
```

The first command revokes the admin option from John for the role `Nurse`. This means that, after the execution of the command, John is still authorized to play the role `Nurse` but he is not authorized to grant others the authorizations to play that role. The second command revokes from role `Healthcare_staff` the authorization to query the name and address of the patients. This means that all the users authorized to play the role of `Healthcare_staff` lose this privilege as well. Finally, the effect of the last command is that `Ann` is no longer authorized to play the role `Cardiologist`.

5.3   ROLE ADMINISTRATION

As we have seen at the beginning of this chapter, the main goal of RBAC is to simplify authorization management. However, large RBAC systems may have hundreds of roles and tens of thousands of users. For example, a case study carried out with Dresdner Bank, a major European bank, resulted in an RBAC system that has about 40,000 users and 1,300 roles [Schaad et al., 2001]. In such kinds of environments the support for decentralized role administration is a fundamental need. Therefore, many proposals have been made of an administrative model for RBAC.

ARBAC97 (Administrative RBAC) [Sandhu et al., 1999] is the first attempt to specify a comprehensive decentralized administrative model for RBAC. The underlying idea is to use roles themselves for role administration. This is achieved by introducing *administrative roles*, to be used for the management of regular roles. Similar to regular roles, administrative roles may be hierarchically organized and may have associated constraints. ARBAC97 is actually a family of models, consisting of URA97, for managing user-role assignment, PRA97, for managing permission-role assignment, and RRA97, for managing role-role assignment, that is, the role hierarchy. Common to all the submodels is the notion of *role range* that identifies a set of roles constituting the administrative domain of an administrative role. Formally, a (closed) role range is denoted as $[x, y] = \{r \in ROLES \mid x \geq r \wedge r \geq y\}$. Ranges may be closed, open and half open.

URA97 defines which administrative roles can assign/revoke which users to which regular roles by means of the relations *can_assign/can_revoke*. *can_assign(ar, prereq, range)* states that a member of the administrative role *ar* (or of one of its senior roles) may assign users to roles denoted by *range* provided that the users satisfy the precondition *prereq*[2]. *prereq* is a role name or a boolean combination of role names. For instance, suppose that *prereq* = $r_1 \vee (r_2 \wedge \neg r_3)$. A user *u* satisfies *prereq* if either *u* is authorized to play r_1 or he/she is authorized to play r_2 and NOT r_3. Roles can be revoked from users through the relation *can_revoke*. The meaning of *can_revoke(ar, range)* is that a member of the administrative role *ar* (or of one of its senior roles) can revoke membership of

---

[2]Alternatively, roles may be explicitly listed instead of being denoted through the range notation.

a user for any role identified by *range*. Note that, when roles are hierarchically organized an issue is whether the revoke operation propagates along the role hierarchy. To allow the maximum flexibility, URA97 supports two different type of revoke operations: *weak* and *strong*. Under weak revocation, role membership revocation is not propagated along the hierarchy, whereas with strong revocation role membership revocation is propagated up in the hierarchy. As an example consider once again the role hierarchy in Figure 5.1 and suppose that Bob is authorized to play the role `Cardiologist`. Now suppose that *can_revoke*(A_1,[`Healthcare_staff`,`Cardiologist`]) has been specified, and that Alice is authorized to play the administrative role A_1. If Alice requires to weakly revoke Bob from the role `Healthcare_staff`, the revoke operation has no effect, since Bob is not an explicit member of `Healthcare_staff`. In contrast, if strong revocation is required, the revoke operation is propagated up in the hierarchy, that is, to the role `Cardiologist`. Clearly, the constraint exists that the administrative role performing the strong revocation has the right to administer all the senior roles to which the revocation is propagated.

PRA97 manages permission-role assignment, by introducing two further relations *can_assignp* and *can_revokep*, which are similar to *can_assign* and *can_revoke* explained above, but they apply to permissions instead of to roles.

The main relation introduced by RRA97 is *can_modify*, which regulates how the role hierarchy may change (i.e., by inserting/deleting an edge) and who can create/delete roles. Different administrative roles may be entitled to modify different portions of the role hierarchy. More precisely, *can_modify*(*ar*, *range*) states that a member of the administrative role *ar* (or of one of its senior roles) can create and delete roles in *range* and can modify relationships between roles in *range*. The constraint exists that none of these operations should introduce a cycle in the hierarchy. Additionally, to ensure that operations performed on a range do not have side effects outside the range, RRA97 requires that all role ranges in the *can_modify* relation are *encapsulated ranges*, that is, each range should have exactly one senior-most role and one junior-most role. To maintain encapsulation of ranges, ARBAC97 poses further constraints on the operations allowed by *can_modify*. More details are discussed by Sandhu et al. [1999].

To summarize, role administration is managed in ARBAC97 by introducing the concepts of administrative role and role range, and a set of relations to perform administrative operations. Some restrictions to these relations have been defined to avoid undesirable side-effects. As a result, many common operations may be performed only by the Security Administrator (SA). Moreover, ARBAC97 does not provide support for the management of administrative roles and the introduced relations that must be centrally managed by the SA. To avoid some of these shortcomings, ARBAC99 [Sandhu and Munawer, 1999] and, later, ARBAC02 [Oh and Sandhu, 2002] were introduced. In particular, ARBAC99 fixes one of the shortcomings of ARBAC97 related to the *prereq* component of the *can_assign* relation. To better understand, suppose that a company has an external consultant that is assigned to the role `Supervisor Project Y` within a project. Membership in this role might be a precondition for further role assignments within the project. However, these further assignments have been conceived for permanent staff only, whereas external consultants should be authorized only to play the Supervisor Project Y role. In ARBAC97 there is no way to prohibit further assignments for the consultant. To address this issue, the ARBAC99 model introduces the notion of *mobile* and *immobile memberships* of users to roles. Immobile assignments of a user to a role means that the user inherits all the authorizations granted to the role, however the fact that he/she has been authorized to play the role does not qualify him/her for any further role assignments. Mobile membership is the standard role membership of ARBAC97. Therefore, in ARBAC99 the external consultant can be given an immobile membership to the supervisor role. ARBAC02 further extends ARBAC97 by adding the notion of *organizational unit*, defining user and permission pools independent from roles and the role hierarchy, as it was in ARBAC97. Assigning a user or permission to a pool is independent from assigning it to a role. However, neither ARBAC99 nor ARBAC02 change the role-role assignment component of ARBAC97.

An alternative model is the SARBAC model (Scoped Administrative RBAC) proposed by Crampton and Loizou [2003], which allows for more flexibility in administrative operations in that some of the operations that should be centrally managed in ARBAC97 (e.g., modification to the introduced relations) may be decentrally managed in SARBAC, to some extent (see [Crampton and Loizou, 2003] for a comprehensive comparison between ARBAC97 and SARBAC). More precisely, they define a family of models for role hierarchy administration (RHA), namely $RHA_1, \ldots, RHA_4$, of increasing complexity and expressive power, where RHA_4 is the SARBAC counterpart of RRA97 in the ARBAC97 model. SARBAC adds to RHA_4 the support for user-role assignment (URA97 in ARBAC97) and permission-role assignment (PRA97 in ARBAC97). Therefore, in what follows, we briefly describe RHA_4 which is the core component of SARBAC. RHA_4 is based on the notion of *administrative scope*, which has some similarities with the notion of encapsulated range in ARBAC97. Administrative scopes are determined by the structure of the role hierarchy. A role r is said to be within the administrative scope of another role a if every path upwards from r goes through a. In other words, any change to r made by a will not have unexpected side effects due to inheritance elsewhere in the hierarchy, since it can be observed only by a and its most senior roles.

Moreover, RHA_4 allows the definition of administrative roles with an associated administrative domain (that is, all the roles in their administrative scopes). For this purpose, a binary relation admin-authority is introduced. If (a, r) belongs to admin-authority, where a is an administrative role, and r is a regular role, it means that a has control over the roles in the administrative scope of r. admin-authority is combined with the role hierarchy into an extended hierarchy consisting of both administrative and regular roles. Differently from ARBAC97, RH_4 also manages additions/deletions to admin-authority, which is equivalent to adding or deleting a corresponding edge in the extended hierarchy. A request to add or delete a tuple in admin-authority may trigger further updates to admin-authority, with the aim of preserving role administrative scopes and avoiding redundancy.

SARBAC extends RH_4 with two further relations ua-constraints and pa-constraints, which are similar to *can-assign* and *can-assignp* in ARBAC97. The model proposed by Crampton and Loizou [2003] has been further refined [Crampton, 2005] to introduce RBAT Role-Based Administration Template, which is a template for the design of administrative models for RBAC.

One of the common points of ARBAC97 and SARBAC is that they use the role hierarchy to define administrative domains. However, this solution is not always the best one in real-life enterprise scenarios. As noticed by Kern et al. [2003], the criteria for defining role hierarchies and administrative domains are not always the same in that administrative domains are mostly defined based on the organizational structure, whereas roles are often defined based on job functions. Therefore, Kern et al. [2003] further extended the notion of organizational unit of ARBAC02, to the more flexible notion of *scope*. A scope is an entity that collects objects according to one or more criteria, which may include the organizational structure, a cost center structure or a combination of several structures. For instance, an administrative domain may contain all roles in one branch of a bank and such roles may not be related at all in the role hierarchy. Therefore, scopes are used by Kern et al. [2003] to define administrative rights for building roles, in contrast to use the role hierarchy. Along the same line is the UARBAC family of administrative models recently proposed by Li and Mao [2007], where administrative domains are defined by specifying constraints on objects (e.g., users, roles) parameter values.

Related to RBAC administration is the problem of identifying a complete, correct, and efficient set of roles, able to make easier authorization administration. This process, known as *role engineering*, is one of the costliest and more difficult tasks in deploying an RBAC system. Similar to database conceptual design, role engineering can be conducted according to two main approaches, i.e., *top-down* and *bottom-up*. According to the top-down approach, the process starts from a detailed analysis of the enterprise business processes, it identifies particular job functions, decomposes them into smaller units, and finally creates roles for these units by associating with them the needed permissions. This is primarily a manual task that requires a lot of effort and a deep knowledge of the business processes, thus requiring the collaboration of security and domain experts. This is one of the main reason why, recently, the bottom-up approach has gained increased popularity. According to this approach, often referred to as *role mining*, data mining techniques are used to automatically discover roles from existing access control related data, in particular the permission assignments to users. As usual, hybrid approaches can exist in which the top-down and bottom-up strategies can be used in different steps in order to refine the set of roles returned by the previous phases. Several different role mining techniques have been proposed so far (e.g., Lu et al. [2008]; Molloy et al. [2008]; Schlegelmilch and Steffens [2005]) to address the role mining problem. One of the key issues is how to measure the goodness of the resulting role set. This has been addressed by Vaidya et al. [2007], through the formal definition of the role mining problem (RMP), i.e., the problem of discovering an optimal set of roles from existing user permissions, and the proof that RMP and its variants are NP-complete. Therefore, it is important to devise heuristic strategies for achieving implementations with reasonable complexity and good results [Ene et al., 2008; Vaidya et al., 2008].

A related key issue is the definition of standard evaluation criteria for the different role mining algorithms proposed so far [Molloy et al., 2009].

5.4   RBAC EXTENSIONS

The RBAC96 model and its standardized versions have been extended in several ways with the aim to address the need of emerging applications and environments. One of the main directions in extending standard RBAC is related to the possibility of modelling context information (cfr. Chapter 1).

A first stream of work in this direction are related to the enhancement of RBAC to capture temporal information and specify temporal dependencies among role activations. The first proposal along this line was Temporal RBAC (TRBAC) [Bertino et al., 2001a], which provides support for temporal and cardinality constraints on the enabling and disabling of roles. The key concept in TRBAC is that roles can be enabled in some time periods and not enabled in others. A disabled role is a role that cannot be activated by users until it is enabled again. To increase the flexibility of the model, TRBAC also provides *role triggers*, that allow one to specify enabling/disabling dependencies among roles. For instance, by using triggers, one can specify that a role must be enabled whenever another role is enabled. A role trigger is characterized by a list of preconditions for the activation of the trigger and an event (i.e., the enabling/disabling of a role). The precondition may include additional events, conditions on the status of a role (e.g., whether a role is enabled or disabled), and constraints on the number of users actually playing a role. An optional clause may be used to defer the execution of the trigger event with respect to the firing of the trigger by a specified amount of time. This has been introduced to manage situations where the disabling is requested for a role which is currently in use in a session. To deal with conflicts that can arise when the simultaneous enabling and disabling of a role is required by different triggers, role enabling and disabling are prioritized and the event with the highest priority takes precedence.

TRBAC has then been extended to Generalized TRBAC (GTRBAC) [Joshi et al., 2005], which provides support for a wider range of temporal constraints, as well as hybrid hierarchy and time-based SoD constraints. Hybrid hierarchy allows to simultaneously model permission inheritance, role activation inheritance, and a combination of the two.

Other RBAC extensions have tried to address the need of capturing location information. This is an urgent need due to the increasing growth of location-based services and mobile applications. Among the proposals in this direction, one of the most comprehensive one is the GEO-RBAC model [Damiani et al., 2007], that integrates RBAC with a spatial model based on the OpenGIS system. GEO-RBAC supports the notion of *spatial role*, that is, a geographically bounded role, activated based on the position of the user. As standard RBAC, GEO-RBAC is actually a family of models. Core GEO-RBAC defines the basic concepts of the model, including the notion of spatial role. Hierarchical GEO-RBAC deals with the support for role hierarchies, whereas Constrained GEO-RBAC supports the specification of SoD constraints for spatial roles. An attempt to combine spatial and temporal context information is the RBAC model proposed by Ray and Toahchoodee [2008].

Another major extension of standard RBAC is represented by P-RBAC, a family of RBAC models providing the support for privacy policies and preferences [Ni et al., 2007]. RBAC has also been extended to address interoperation issues in multidomain application environments, where parties with different set of access control requirements and models must cooperate [Shafiq et al., 2005].

CHAPTER 6

Emerging Trends in Access Control

Computer science is a fascinating field, and one of the main reasons for that is its rapid, continuous evolution. This is true also for access control, which is characterized by frequent new developments to be able to answer the needs of new scenarios and new kinds of data. This trend is particularly evident in recent years, due to a variety of new developments, most of them arising in the field of Web data management. In this chapter, we focus our attention on some of the most relevant research trends in the field of access control. The first is related to cloud computing that has highly impacted the way data management services are provided over the Internet. The second is related to the protection of data streams, and the third is how access control has been impacted by the Web 2.0 revolution. Finally, we conclude the chapter by discussing further research directions in the field of access control.

6.1 ACCESS CONTROL UNDER THE DATABASE AS A SERVICE MODEL

In the era of cloud computing, resources and applications are provided as a service over the Internet [Hayes, 2008]. Main benefits of this paradigm are well known and range from cost reduction (users pay only for the services they use and not for their development, installation, and maintenance), scalability, better quality of service, and more effective allocation of internal resources. Gartner Inc. predicts that by 2012, 80% of Fortune 1000 enterprises will pay for some cloud-computing services, while 30% of them will pay for cloud-computing infrastructures[1].

In this scenario, an important role is played by data management services. In this respect, a new emerging option is represented by the *Database as a Service* (DbaaS) paradigm [Ferrari, 2009b]. DbaaS is regulated by the same principles as Software as a Service (SaaS) and basically means the delivery of the typical functionalities of a database management system in the cloud. DbaaS has attracted the interests of many vendors (e.g., IBM and Microsoft, as well as small innovators such as EnterpriseDB, LongJump, and Elastra).

Under the DbaaS model, there is a shift from the traditional client-server architecture, where the data owner directly manages the DMS and answers user queries, to a third party architecture, where data owners are no longer totally responsible for data management. Rather, they outsource

---

[1]http://www.gartner.com.

their data (or portions of them) to one or more *data service providers* (or *publishers*) that provide data management services.

However, one of the most serious obstacles to the widespread use of DbaaS is related to the security and privacy of the managed data. Indeed, data outsourcing may be perceived by the data owner as a sort of "loss of control" over its data, unless one can have strong guarantees on the security and privacy of the outsourced data. The challenge is therefore how to ensure properties such as confidentiality, integrity, authenticity, and privacy, even if data are not directly managed by the owner but by a third party. Among all the above-mentioned properties, those related to access control are confidentiality and integrity. However, up to now almost no research proposal considers integrity requirements arising from updates at the publisher side. They assume an architecture where data updates are only performed by the owner that periodically updates the data and send them to publishers. Users can query the data managed by the publisher but not modify them. Therefore, in what follows, we will focus only on confidentiality issues. We refer the interested reader to Ferrari [2009b] for a survey of the state of the art addressing the other security and privacy properties.

Confidentiality issues in the DbaaS model can be addressed in a very simple way; that is, by assuming a trusted publisher, who is a publisher that always operates according to the access control policies stated by the data owner. Under this simple model, the publisher hosts a trusted reference monitor in charge of enforcing access control according to the authorizations specified by the data owner. However, this assumption is not realistic in real world scenarios. This is especially true for Web-based systems that can be easily attacked and penetrated. Additionally, verifying that a publisher is trusted is a very costly operation. Therefore, the research has focused on the development of techniques ensuring confidentiality of the outsourced data in the presence of an *untrusted publisher* that can, for instance, release the data it manages to unauthorized subjects. An important issue is also how to trade-off between the obtained confidentiality guarantees and the efficiency/scalability of the devised solution.

Under the DbaaS model, confidentiality has a twofold meaning. The first (referred to as *confidentiality with respect to the users* [Carminati et al., 2005]) is the standard definition of confidentiality (cfr. Chapter 1) – that is, protecting data from unauthorized read operations by end users. This means ensuring that each user receives from the publisher only the data authorized by the data owner. The second, referred to as *confidentiality with respect to the publishers* [Carminati et al., 2005], means protecting data from read operations by publishers, since no assumption is made on their trustworthiness. Confidentiality with respect to publishers has been widely investigated by many researchers. Almost all the solutions proposed so far exploit cryptographic techniques to achieve it. The idea is that data are encrypted by the owner before these are delivered to the publisher. Since the publisher does not receive any decryption key, it is not able to read the data it manages. The most challenging issue in this scenario is to develop query processing techniques for encrypted data. Several techniques have been proposed for this purpose, which differ on the types of queries they support and on the considered data model.

For instance, the work by Agrawal et al. [2004] proposes an order-preserving encryption scheme for numeric data that allows any comparison operation to be directly applied on encrypted data. An alternative approach [Hacigümüs et al., 2002; Hacigümüs et al., 2004] works for relational data and exploits partitioning techniques and privacy homomorphisms. Privacy homomorphisms are encryption transformations that allow one to calculate arithmetic operations directly on encrypted data. Partitioning techniques are used to perform selection queries over encrypted relational data, whereas homomorphic encryption is used to manage aggregate queries over encrypted tuples. To perform selection queries the basic idea is to divide the domain of each attribute in a relation R into distinguished partitions, with an associated id. Then, for each tuple t in R, the owner sends the publisher the corresponding encrypted tuple, together with the ids of the partitions to which t's attribute values belong to. These ids are used by the publisher to answer selection queries over encrypted data, provided that a user, before submitting a query to a publisher, rewrites it in terms of partition ids. Clearly, storing the data in encrypted format entails significant performance penalties during query processing, that require ad-hoc query optimization strategies to be developed [Hacigümüs et al., 2005]. Other techniques (e.g., [Song et al., 2000]) have been developed for textual data and allow keyword-based searches over textual encrypted data.

Other works have developed techniques for querying XML encrypted data. Brinkman et al. [2004] developed an encryption technique for XML, based on the work of Song et al. [2000], exploiting its tree structure. The approach is based on the storage of XML data into relational tables, and therefore it does not protect structural information. This drawback is overcome by the work of Wang and Lakshmanan [2006], where a set of *security constraints* is specified by the data owner to state which nodes of the XML documents should be encrypted to prevent their access from the publishers or any outsider attacker. Efficiency of query processing is improved through the use of metadata to be stored on the data provider site, whose presence does not compromise the security of the system, which has been proved robust to a number of different attacks.

All the works presented so far consider only confidentiality with respect to the publisher, therefore they do not consider a scenario where the data owner can specify authorizations granting different users the right to see different portions of the outsourced data. In contrast, this issue is addressed by Carminati et al. [2005] and Miklau and Suciu [2003] for XML data. Both works exploit encryption to enforce the owner access control policies. Different keys are used to encrypt different nodes of the XML document, on the basis of the specified access control policies. Keys are then transmitted by the data owner to the users based on the access control policies they satisfy. More precisely, Miklau and Suciu [2003] defined a policy language based on XQuery to specify access control policies. Access to a node is granted based on the possession of specific keys and the fact that a user knows the value of specific attributes within the document (for instance, a user should know the value of the DNASignature attribute to access the whole analysis element). The XML Encryption W3C recommendation is used as the encryption format. According to the architecture proposed by Miklau and Suciu [2003], each user downloads a copy of the encrypted data and selectively accesses them on the basis of the keys he/she holds. One of the main drawbacks of this approach is that the user should know structural information of the original XML document to perform the query. Additionally, each user downloads the whole published document even if he/she can access a limited portion of it. Other important issues that are not addressed by Miklau and Suciu [2003] are related to key management. Indeed, the feasibility of any cryptographic-based solution is related to the efficiency of key management both in terms of the number of keys to be generated and the overhead implied by data or access control policy updates. To address some of these issues, a different approach is taken by Carminati et al. [2005]. Similar to Miklau and Suciu [2003], confidentiality with respect to the user is obtained by encrypting different portions of the original XML document with different keys, on the basis of the owner access control policies. Policies are specified using an XML-based language that allows the specification of credential-based and content-based fine-grained access control policies on the managed data. However, to limit the number of keys to be generated, the system adopts an hierarchical key assignment scheme [Bertino et al., 2002] that requires to permanently store, in the worst case, a number of keys linear in the number of specified access control policies. To cope with the heterogeneous nature of XML data, the system proposed in Carminati et al. [2005] makes use of two different encryption strategies, inspired by Hacigümüs et al. [2002] and Song et al. [2000], respectively. In particular, an approach similar to the one proposed by Song et al. [2000] is used to encrypt textual data, as well as to encrypt document tagnames. In contrast, for non-textual data, the method proposed by Hacigümüs et al. [2002] is used and adapted to XML data, and to documents encrypted with multiple keys. All the metadata needed by the publishers to query encrypted data, as well as the document encryption itself, are wrapped into an XML document, called SE-Enc (Security-Enhanced Encryption) document. Main benefits of the proposed solution is that it is robust to data dictionary attacks both at the schema and document content level. A query translator module (see Carminati et al. [2005] for more details) is in charge of translating user queries into ciphered queries to be submitted to publishers. Modifications to the SE-Enc documents due to policy and/or document updates are incrementally managed, that is, by changing only the portions of the SE-Enc documents that are really affected by the update operations.

6.2 ACCESS CONTROL FOR DATA STREAM MANAGEMENT SYSTEMS

Today there are many scenarios (e.g., battle field and network monitoring, telecommunications, financial monitoring, sensor networks, Web searches, and so on) where data arrive in the form of high-speed streams [Aggarwal, 2007; Golab and Özsu, 2003] that should be managed and protected on the fly. Existing access control models and systems have typically assumed a passive scenario. These approaches should therefore be redesigned to be applied to Data Stream Management Systems (DSMSs). The development of an access control system for DSMSs is further complicated by the fact that, differently from relational DMSs, a standard model and query language for DSMSs have not yet emerged. Therefore, it is difficult to develop a system for securing data streams that is independent from the target stream engine.

Access control for data streams is a new research area; as such, there are only a few proposals dealing with this issue. In general, three are the main strategies that can be adopted to enforce access control over data streams: *pre-processing*, *post-processing*, and *query rewriting*. Pre-processing means that the streams are pruned from the unauthorized tuples before entering the query processor. Clearly, the main drawback of this simple strategy is that it works well only for very simple access control models with a limited policy language. For instance, it is not possible to support authorizations on views if a pre-processing strategy is adopted. In contrast, post-processing first executes the original user query, then, it prunes from the result the non-authorized tuples, before delivering the resulting stream to the user. Like pre-processing, this strategy has the drawback that it does not support access control policies defined over portions of combined streams. In addition, it may waste computation, since queries are evaluated even if they are denied by the specified access control policies. The third way is query rewriting, a technique widely used in many other contexts (e.g., relational DMSs, XML data), which consists of rewriting the user query on the basis of the specified authorizations in such a way that the query returns only authorized data. Access control is therefore applied at query definition time, that is, when queries are registered into the system.

A model adopting the post-processing strategy, is the Owner extended RBAC (OxRBAC) model [Lindner and Meier, 2006]. Post-processing is enforced by applying the SecFilter operator at the stream resulting from the evaluation of a query, to filter out output tuples that do not satisfy the access control rules. As mentioned before, the main disadvantages of post-processing is that it may cause computation waste and it may only support a limited set of access control policies.

In contrast, the framework proposed by Carminati et al. [2010] uses query rewriting to enforce access control. It is an attempt to develop a powerful access control system while, at the same time, be as independent as possible from the target DSMS. The framework supports a flexible role-based access control model, where objects to be protected are queries over data streams. Two types of privileges are supported: a read privilege, for operations such as selection, projection and join that require reading the content of a stream, and aggregate privileges, for operations such as min, max, count, avg, and sum. To cope with the temporal dimension of data streams, the model supports general temporal constraints that allow access to data during a given time bound, and window temporal constraints that support aggregate operations within a specified time window. The system acts as a middleware able to deploy rewritten queries into a set of different DSMSs. To cope with the lack of standardization, a core query model has been defined, on which the proposed access control mechanism is based, which formalizes the set of query operators that are common to most of the stream query languages proposed so far. Query rewriting exploits a set of secure operators (namely, `Secure Read`, `Secure View`, `Secure Join`, and `Secure Aggregate`) that filter out from the results of the corresponding (not secure) operators those tuples/attributes that are not accessible according to the specified access control policies. Since query rewriting is based on the defined core query model, it is independent from the target stream engine. The deployment module is then in charge of translating the results of query rewriting into the languages supported by the various DSMSs. The performance study conducted on the prototype implementation [Cao et al., 2009] measuring the overhead of query rewriting shows the feasibility of the developed techniques and its performance gain with respect to post-processing.

A different approach has been proposed by Nehme et al. [2009]. Differently from the Carminati et al. [2010] proposal, authorizations are specified by the owner of the device producing the data stream, rather than by the SA of the DSMS. In this way, a user is able to specify how the DSMS has to access the information (e.g., location, health conditions). Therefore, this proposal is related to both privacy and access control, whereas Carminati et al. [2010] proposal focuses on access control only. Since authorizations are specified by the data stream owner, they are not stored in the DSMS, rather they are encoded via security constraints (called *security punctuations*) and embedded into the data streams themselves. A set of operators is then defined to enforce constraints modeled by security punctuations.

6.3   ACCESS CONTROL IN THE WEB 2.0 ERA

Today one of the most relevant phenomena in Computer Science is represented by Web 2.0 related technologies that have made possible social computing services, such as blogs, wikis, and social networks. Such tools are rapidly transforming the Web from a simple tool for publishing textual data into a complex collaborative knowledge management system to be used both for personal purposes and for business activities. This later trend is known as Enterprise 2.0 [McAfee, 2006], that is, the use of Web 2.0 technologies within the intranet, to allow for more spontaneous, knowledge-based collaborations.

One of the main witnesses of this new trend is represented by Online Social Networks (OSNs), platforms that allow people to publish details about themselves and to connect to other members of the network through friendship or other kinds of links. Recently, the popularity of OSNs is increasing significantly. For example, Facebook now claims to have more than 400 million active users[2]. The existence of OSNs that include person-specific information creates both interesting opportunities and challenges, one of the most significant is related to data protection. In what follows, we discuss the main security challenges and relevant research proposals, by focusing on access control.

6.3.1   OSN ACCESS CONTROL REQUIREMENTS

An access control mechanism for OSNs needs to consider various issues specific to social networks. As far as the access control policy specification language is concerned, today there is a consensus that access control in OSNs should be *relationship-based*, that is, it should provide support for the specification of policies granting access on the shared resources on the basis of user relationships, their types and depth. An example of relationship-based policy is the one authorizing access to my pictures only to my friends and the direct friends of my friends. Another key parameter that may be useful in determining who is authorized to access OSNs resources is *trust* [Jøsang et al., 2007]. For instance, one can differently trust one's direct friends and therefore would be willing

---

[2]http://www.facebook.com/press/info.php?statistics. Retrieved on March 4, 2010.

to share a confidential resource only with the most trustworthy ones. This requirement cannot be supported by relationship-based access control only. Therefore, access control policies for OSNs should also support constraints on the minimum trust level of a relationship. A further requirement is related to access administration in that OSNs require revisions for the conventional ownership-based administration policy traditionally adopted by DMSs (see Chapter 1). For example, assume that a picture is uploaded in the social network, and suppose that the owner of the photo tags some other users on the photo. Tagged users may have some rights on the photo (e.g., removing the tags about them or controlling the release of the photo to other users) even if they are not the owner of the photo. This requires devising *collaborative policies* for access control and authorization administration.

Other relevant issues are related to access control enforcement. Besides the traditional efficiency issues related to the overhead of access control, there are other interesting issues related to the confidentiality and privacy guarantees connected to access control enforcement in OSNs. Indeed, if we simply transpose the model used by traditional DMSs to the OSN environment, this means that the OSN manager should host both access authorizations and the reference monitor. This implies that users have to completely delegate the control of their data to the OSN manager, by simply stating how data must be released to other network nodes. Therefore, OSN users have to fully trust the OSN manager. However, the increasing privacy concerns about how these systems manage personal information (see, for instance, Berteau [2007]) lead us to believe that a centralized access control solution is not the most appropriate one in the OSN scenario. Indeed, social network participants would like to have more and more control over their data. Decentralization [Yeung et al., 2009] can provide answers to these issues, making the network participants themselves able to evaluate and enforce their own access control policies. However, devising a fully decentralized solution is not easy since access control decisions rely on some information (i.e., the existence of specific paths in the network) that it is not easy to locally manage.

6.3.2   PROPOSED SOLUTIONS

In what follows, we review the main proposals addressing access control for OSNs.

Ali et al. [2007] proposed a mandatory access control model, where subject security levels are determined based on trust. Access control is enforced according to a challenge-response protocol. This proposal has the drawback that it only considers direct relationships for policy specification, which greatly limits the access control policies a user may enforce. Subsequently, Villegas et al. [2008] extended the model to use the distance between the owner and the requestor in the access control decision. More precisely, users that are directly or indirectly connected to the resource owner are classified into three adjacent zones: "acceptance" zones, whose access requests will be immediately accepted; "attestation" zones, whose access requests require a further evaluation to gain access, and "rejection" zones, whose access requests will be immediately rejected. As a consequence, confidentiality requirements on resources are specified in terms of two distances, called trusted distances, delimiting the three zones.

In contrast, the D-FOAF (Friend-of-a-Friend) system [Kruk et al., 2006] is primarily a FOAF-based distributed identity management system for OSNs, where access control and trust delegation management are provided as additional services. D-FOAF enforces relationship-based access control. However, a weak point in this approach is that it does not prevent the forging of fake relationships. Since access control is relationship-based, this may imply possible unauthorized accesses to take place, in that a user may forge a fake relationship to establish a path between him/her an the resource owner in order to get unauthorized access to one of its resources.

Another effort to enforce access control in OSNs has been proposed by Ando et al. [2008]. The idea is to create a peer-to-peer network on the basis of the relationships existing in a given social network such that two peers are connected only if there exists a relationship between them in the underlying OSN. Therefore, access control can be performed directly by the owner of the resource, since each node communicates directly with the requesting node. Trust is not a parameter for the access control decision.

In the model presented by Tootoonchian et al. [2009], authorizations are encoded into access control lists (ACLs), called social ACLs, that contain, for each resource, the identifiers of users authorized to access it, as well as the relationships users must be involved in to gain access. The system presented by Baden et al. [2009] exploits cryptographic primitives to enforce group-based access control in OSNs. The underlying idea is that users are able to organize their friends into groups, and assign permissions to them by means of ACLs. As this proposal considers a social network model similar to Facebook, groups generation does not take into account relationship types and trust. The main contribution of this proposal are the cryptographic primitives exploited to enforce the authorizations in ACLs.

The work of Fong et al. [2009] analyzes the access control mechanism of Facebook, with the aim of enhancing it. The model supports three further policy types, besides access control policies. Search and traversal policies have been defined by taking into consideration that Facebook allows one to look for new users in the social network by accessing: (a) some parts of the user's profiles, and (b) the users' friend lists. Fong et al. [2009] also support communication policies, making users able to state who is authorized to initiate a given type of communication with him/her.

Up until now, the most comprehensive access control solution we are aware of is the one proposed by Carminati et al. [2009b], where access control requirements can be expressed in terms of type, depth and trust level of the network relationships. To avoid relationship forging, relationships are certified. As far as access control enforcement is concerned, the system exploits a client-based approach, according to which the requestor must provide the resource owner with a proof (that is, a path in the network) of being authorized to access the requested resource. Main benefits of this protocol is that the burden of access control enforcement is mainly on the user who requests the access. The performance evaluation carried out on the prototype implementation shows the feasibility of the approach for the Enterprise 2.0 scenario.

The widespread use of Semantic Web technologies to model OSNs has also impacted access control. Indeed, these technologies allow to provide much richer social network data (e.g., representing different kinds of relationships among users and resources) and, on these semantically enriched social networks, more flexible and expressive access control requirements may be specified and enforced, as shown by recent work (see, e.g., Carminati et al. [2009a]; Elahi et al. [2008]). For example, Elahi et al. [2008] proposed a semantic framework based on OWL - Web Ontology Language [Patel-Schneider et al., 2004] - for defining different access rights exploiting the relationships between the individuals and the community. In contrast, Carminati et al. [2009a] proposed an extensible fine grained access control model based on OWL and SWRL (Semantic Web Rule Language [Horrocks et al., 2004]) where social network-related information are encoded by means of an ontology. The main advantage of this is that relationships among many different social network concepts can be naturally represented using OWL. Furthermore, by using reasoning, many inferences about such relationships could be done automatically and exploited for access control enforcement. Besides access control policies, the system provides *filtering policies*, by which OSN users may specify which data have to be filtered out when themselves or other users (e.g., their children) browse social network resources.

6.4   FURTHER RESEARCH DIRECTIONS IN ACCESS CONTROL

Besides the research trends described in the previous sections, there are additional new research areas in the field of access control, where we foresee interesting developments in the near future.

- *Trust computation*. As we have seen in Section 6.3, trust is one of the key parameters on which access control decisions should be based in an open environment like the Web. Today, there is a general consensus on the fact that there does not exist a general definition of trust, and that trust evaluation mainly depends on the purposes for which trust has to be used. For instance, in peer-to-peer environments trust is mainly related to quality of services, whereas in recommendation systems trust is a measure of the expertise of a user on particular topics. When dealing with access control, trust has a completely different flavor. When is a user trusted? Trust should be a measure of the compliance of the user actions to the specified access control policies. Related to this is the issue of trust computation. This is a crucial issue that has not been so far deeply investigated, in that assigning a wrong trust value to a potential malicious user could imply unauthorized releasing of information. Several different methods can be devised, such as those based on logging user activities with respect to the release of protected resources, or applying data mining techniques to discover *patterns* that may help in determining trusted and untrusted users. Further, it is important that, whichever mechanism is used to determine the trustworthiness of a user, such mechanism is *privacy-preserving*, that is, the techniques used for trust computation should not reveal confidential/private information about the involved users. Up to now, we are aware of very few works addressing this issue (see, e.g., Nin et al. [2009]).

- *Access control and privacy for mobile users and location-based services.* Users are increasingly mobile, and devices like smartphones are more and more available to a wider user population. Location-based social networks, like Foursquare, Gowalla, Brightkite and Google Buzz, are currently among the fastest growing new mobile services. All of these services have one thing in common, that is, encouraging users to share their current location with the rest of the world. This may serve for a variety of purposes, such as, to match a user with a place, an event, or a local group in which to socialize, to provide the users some customized services, on the basis of their location, or to coordinate hazards and disaster aid activities. To motivate users in releasing their locations, some location-based services, such as Foursquare, have started rewarding the disclosure of location-based information with virtual badges and real-world discounts. However, the precise disclosure of location information may have serious implications on user privacy and security. First of all, if you disclose your location, you are telling people where you are not: for instance, at home. A new site, PleaseRobMe, plays on this theme and displays real-time updates from Foursquare users who broadcast their check-ins on Twitter. According to their developers the goal of the website is to raise some awareness on the potential dangers connected to the disclosure of location-based information to make people think about how they use location-based services and their potential risks. Besides robberies, there are also other reasons that might prevent a user to always disclose his/her location. For instance, you might not want to tell your future employer that your spent a lot of week nights at the local bar or that you have frequently made visit to a certain hospital in the last month. The success of location-based networks/services will greatly depend on making users feel safe when using these services [Decker, 2008]. Different techniques have been so far proposed for protecting against the disclosure of location information in location-based services, such as for instance cryptographic-based and perturbation-based techniques [Bonchi and Ferrari, 2010; Giannotti and Pedreschi, 2008]. However, the development of a general-purpose scalable and efficient solution relying on a realistic adversary model and able to trade-off between quality of services and privacy guarantees is still an open issue.

- *Going beyond traditional access control and privacy-preserving mechanisms.* In the TV show Fast Future Forward, aired by CNN on January 1, 2010, the anchor-woman asked the panel of futurists: "Which major challenge are we going to have to deal with 10 years out?" The answer was: "We'll have to completely reverse our orientation to privacy. The reality is that we don't have privacy anymore: you use your cell phone, you drive your car, you go on-line, and it's gone." Few days later Facebook founder Mark Zuckerberg in a interview with the weblog TechCrunch argued that "Privacy is no longer a social norm, because people have really gotten comfortable not only sharing more information, but more openly and with more people. That social norm is just something that has evolved over time."

Although the debate on the vanishing of privacy and confidentiality is going on for years, it is true that the advent of social computing services and the deployment of sensors and computing devices in almost all the environments have exacerbated the problem. However, many people do not agree with Zuckerberg's view and still recognize the importance of a transparent, trustworthy, and fair management of digital information, where the risks connected to information disclosure cannot be eliminated but they are kept under control. However, it should be recognized that concepts such as privacy and confidentiality have evolved over time and that accessible social networking technology changes communication between people in a way similar to, if not as intensely as, the introduction of the telephone and the printing press. However, most people using social networks are not totally aware of the risks connected with sharing personal information on a platform accessible by million of users. Most of them join the network under the belief their information could be shared just between trusted friends. Others may be willing to disclose their personal information if this gives them some rewards (for instance in terms of better services or in terms of an improvement of their social relations). What is needed is to rethink the way access control is enforced through the definition of trustworthy technologies that make each single user able to decide with whom and under which conditions to share his/her personal information and resources. Additionally, we need user friendly tools that make average Web users able to understand how they can protect their resources. Indeed, empirical analysis on available OSNs show that privacy settings are perceived as cumbersome and their use poorly communicated (see for instance [Bonneau and Preibusch, 2009] for a detailed analysis of 45 major OSNs). A step in this direction is represented by FaceCloak [Luo et al., 2009], an architecture that allows a user to customize the obtained privacy guarantees by deciding which information he/she wants to safeguard and which to leave as it was, based on his/her own judgment of the value of privacy. Private information are protected not only from unauthorized users but also from the social networking site. This is achieved by providing fake information to the social networking site and by storing sensitive information in encrypted form on a separate server.

Another important research challenge is how to make a user able to understand the effects of the access control policies he/she specifies, in terms of authorized users and in terms of the risk of unauthorized disclosure of information. For instance, if we consider again the OSN scenario, access rules usually specify authorized users by stating constraints on the relationships in the OSN (cfr. Section 6.3). Even in small social networks, one can hardly understand which users are actually authorized even by simple access rules such as "friends of my friends" due to the many relationships that users can establish. This possible loss of control generates serious potential risks of unauthorized information flow. Therefore, there is the need of estimating the potential risks that may result from the access rules specified in OSNs, so the users are fully aware of the possible effects of their decisions in specifying access rules.

- *Information accountability.* The main goal of any access control mechanism has been so far to prevent information transfer beyond certain boundaries (e.g., the organization owner of the information, a set of trusted users, all the users that need it to perform their job function). However, this model does not completely fit today's open and interconnected world, where information can be easily transferred, aggregated, and linked with other information sources to infer sensitive information. As stated before, there is the need to go beyond the way access control has been performed so far. A promising possibility is represented by *information accountability* [Weitzner et al., 2008]. Building an infrastructure on support of information accountability means, instead of trying to prevent each unauthorized access to information, making misuses visible and subjects accountable for such misuses. This can be achieved by making information usage transparent, so it is possible to determine whether a use is appropriate or not under a given set of constraints. The development of a technical infrastructure on support of information accountability is still an open issue.

Bibliography

C. Aggarwal, editor. *Data Streams – Models and Algorithms*. Springer, 2007. 80

R. Agrawal, J. Kiernan, R. Srikant, and Y. Xu. Order Preserving Encryption for Numeric Data. In *Proc. ACM SIGMOD Int. Conf. on Management of Data*, pages 563–574, 2004. ISBN 1-58113-859-8. DOI: 10.1145/1007568.1007632 79

R. Agrawal, P. Bird, T. Grandison, J. Kiernan, S. Logan, and W. Rjaibi. Extending Relational Database Systems to Automatically Enforce Privacy Policies. In *Proc. 21st Int. Conf. on Data Engineering*, pages 1013–1022, 2005. DOI: 10.1109/ICDE.2005.64 2

R. Ahad, J. Davis, S. Gower, P. Lyngbaek, A. Marynowski, and E. Onuegbe. Supporting Access Control in an Object-Oriented Database Language. In *Advances in Database Technology, Proc. 3rd Int. Conf. on Extending Database Technology*, pages 184–200, 1992. ISBN 3-540-55270-7. DOI: 10.1007/BFb0032431 38

M.A. Al-Kahtani and R. Sandhu. Rule-Based RBAC with Negative Authorization. In *Proc. Annual Computer Security Applications Conference*, pages 405–415, 2004. ISBN 0-7695-2252-1. DOI: 10.1109/CSAC.2004.32 27

K. Alghathbar, C. Farkas, and D. Wijesekera. Securing UML Information Flow using FlowUML. *Journal of Research and Practice in Information Technology* 38(1):229–238, 2006. 60

B. Ali, W. Villegas, and M. Maheswaran. A Trust based Approach for Protecting User Data in Social Networks. In *Proc. Conf. of the Center for Advanced Studies on Collaborative Research*, pages 288–293, 2007. DOI: 10.1145/1321211.1321251 83

K. Ando, A. Fukagai, K. Ohshima, and M. Terada. DHT Network with Link Access Control Using a Social Network. In *Proc. 2008 Int. Symposium on Applications and the Internet*, pages 18–25, 2008. ISBN 978-0-7695-3297-4. DOI: 10.1109/SAINT.2008.23 84

V. Atluri and A. Gal. An Authorization Model for Temporal and Derived Data: Securing Information Portals. *ACM Trans. Information & Syst. Sec.*, 5(1):62–94, 2002. ISSN 1094-9224. DOI: 10.1145/504909.504912 30

V. Atluri, S. Jajodia, and E. Bertino. Alternative Correctness Criteria for Concurrent Execution of Transactions in Multilevel Secure Databases. *IEEE Trans. Knowl. and Data Eng.*, 8(5):839–854, 1996. DOI: 10.1109/69.542034 59

R. Baden, A. Bender, N. Spring, B. Bhattacharjee, and D. Starin. Persona: an Online Social Network with User-defined Privacy. In *Proc. ACM Int. Conf. on Data Communication*, pages 135–146, 2009. ISBN 978-1-60558-594-9. DOI: 10.1145/1592568.1592585 84

D. Bell and L. LaPadula. Secure Computer Systems: Unified Exposition and Multics Interpretation. Technical report, Hanscom Air Force Base, Bedford, MA, 1975. 50

S. Berteau. Facebook's Misrepresentation of Beacon's Threat to Privacy: Tracking Users who Opt out or are not Logged in. *CA Security Advisor Research Blog*, 2007. http://community.ca.com/blogs/securityadvisor/archive/2007/11/29/facebook-s-misrepresentation-of-beacon-s-threat-to-privacy-tracking-users-who-opt-out-or-are-not-logged-in.aspx 83

E. Bertino and E. Ferrari. Secure and Selective Dissemination of XML Documents. *ACM Trans. Information & Syst. Sec.*, 5(3):290–331, 2002. DOI: 10.1145/545186.545190 44

E. Bertino and L.M. Haas. Views and Security in Distributed Database Management Systems. In *Advances in Database Technology, Proc. 1st Int. Conf. on Extending Database Technology*, pages 155–169, 1988. ISBN 3-540-19074-0. DOI: 10.1007/3-540-19074-0_52 26

E. Bertino and R. S. Sandhu. Database Security: Concepts, Approaches, and Challenges. *IEEE Trans. on Dependable and Secure Comput.*, 2(1):2–19, 2005. DOI: 10.1109/TDSC.2005.9 1, 27

E. Bertino and H. Weigand. An Approach to Authorization Modeling in Object-oriented Database Systems. *Data & Knowl. Eng.*, 12(1):1–29, 1994. DOI: 10.1016/0169-023X(94)90020-5 38

E. Bertino, P. Samarati, and S. Jajodia. An Extended Authorization Model for Relational Databases. *IEEE Trans. Knowl. and Data Eng.*, 9(1):85–101, 1997. ISSN 1041-4347. DOI: 10.1109/69.567051 21, 26, 27

E. Bertino, C. Bettini, E Ferrari, and P. Samarati. An Access Control Model Supporting Periodicity Constraints and Temporal Reasoning. *ACM Trans. Database Syst.*, 23(3):231–285, 1998a. DOI: 10.1145/293910.293151 8, 26, 29, 30

E. Bertino, S. De Capitani Di Vimercati, E. Ferrari, and P. Samarati. Exception-based Information Flow Control in Object-oriented Systems. *ACM Trans. Information & Syst. Sec.*, 1(1):26–65, 1998b. ISSN 1094-9224. DOI: 10.1145/290163.290167 59, 60

E. Bertino, P.A. Bonatti, E. Ferrari, and M.L. Sapino. Temporal Authorization Bases: from Specification to Integration. *J. Computer Security*, 8(4):309–353, 2000a. 8, 30

E. Bertino, F. Buccafurri, E. Ferrari, and P. Rullo. A Logic-based Approach for Enforcing Access Control. *J. Computer Security*, 8(2/3):109–139, 2000b. 7, 38

E. Bertino, P.A. Bonatti, and E. Ferrari. TRBAC: A Temporal Role-based Access Control Model. *ACM Trans. Information & Syst. Sec.*, 4(3):191–233, 2001a. ISSN 1094-9224. DOI: 10.1145/501978.501979 8, 65, 74

E. Bertino, S. Castano, and E. Ferrari. Securing XML Documents with Author-X. *IEEE Internet Computing*, 5(3):21–31, 2001b. DOI: 10.1109/4236.935172 27, 42, 44

E. Bertino, B. Catania, and E. Ferrari. A Nested Transaction Model for Multilevel Secure Database Management Systems. *ACM Trans. Information & Syst. Sec.*, 4(4):321–370, 2001c. ISSN 1094-9224. DOI: 10.1145/503339.503340 58

E. Bertino, B. Carminati, and E. Ferrari. A Temporal Key Management Scheme for Secure Broadcasting of XML Documents. In *Proc. 9th ACM Conf. on Computer and Communication Security*, pages 31–40, 2002. DOI: 10.1145/586110.586116 45, 80

E. Bertino, B. Catania, E. Ferrari, and P. Perlasca. A Logical Framework for Reasoning about Access Control Models. *ACM Trans. Information & Syst. Sec.*, 6(1):71–127, 2003. ISSN 1094-9224. DOI: 10.1145/605434.605437 7, 29

E. Bertino, E. Ferrari, and A. Perego. A General Framework for Web Content Filtering. *World Wide Web J.*, 2009. DOI: 10.1007/s11280-009-0073-5 27, 29

J. Biskup and S. Wortmann. Towards a Credential-based Implementation of Compound Access Control Policies. In *Proc. 9th ACM Symposium on Access Control Models and Technologies*, pages 31–40, 2004. DOI: 10.1145/990036.990042 41

M. Blanton. Authentication. In L. Liu and M.T. Özsu, editors, *Encyclopedia of Database Systems*, Springer, page 180. 2009. DOI: 10.1007/978-0-387-39940-9 3

P.A. Bonatti and D. Olmedilla. Rule-based Policy Representation and Reasoning for the Semantic Web. In *Reasoning Web, Third International Summer School*, pages 240–268, 2007. DOI: 10.1007/978-3-540-74615-7_4 7

F. Bonchi and E. Ferrari, editors. *Privacy-aware Knowledge Discovery: Novel Applications and New Techniques*. Chapman and Hall/CRC Press, 2010. 2, 86

J. Bonneau and S. Preibusch. The Privacy Jungle: on the Market for Data Protection in Social Networks. In *Proc. 8th Workshop on the Economics of Information Security*, 2009. 87

T. Bray, J. Paoli, C.M. Sperberg-McQueen, E. Maler, and F. Yergeau. Extensible Markup Language (XML) 1.0 (Third Edition), W3C Recommendation. Technical report, W3C, 2004. URL http://www.w3.org/TR/2004/REC-xml-20040204. 39

R. Brinkman, L. Feng, J. Doumen, P.H. Hartel, and W. Jonker. Efficient Tree Search in Encrypted Data. *Information Security J.*, 13:14–21, 2004. DOI: 10.1201/1086/44530.13.3.20040701/83065.3 79

R.K. Burns. Referential Secrecy. *Proc. 11th IEEE Symposium on Security & Privacy*, page 133, 1990. DOI: 10.1109/RISP.1990.63845 56

J.W. Byun and N. Li. Purpose based Access Control for Privacy Protection in Relational Database Systems. *VLDB J.*, 17(4):603–619, 2008. DOI: 10.1007/s00778-006-0023-0 2

J. Cao, B. Carminati, E. Ferrari, and K.L. Tan. ACStream: Enforcing Access Control over Data Streams. In *Proc. 25th Int. Conf. on Data Engineering*, pages 1495–1498, 2009. DOI: 10.1109/ICDE.2009.25 81

B. Carminati and E. Ferrari. AC-XML Documents: Improving the Performance of a Web Access Control Module. In *Proc. 10th ACM Symposium on Access Control Models and Technologies*, pages 67–76. ACM, 2005. ISBN 1-59593-045-0. DOI: 10.1145/1063979.1063993 47

B. Carminati and E. Ferrari. Access Control and Privacy in Web-based Social Networks. *Int. Journal of Web Information Systems*, 4(4):395–415, 2008. DOI: 10.1108/17440080810919468 8

B. Carminati, E. Ferrari, and E. Bertino. Securing XML Data in Third-party Distribution Systems. In *Proc. 14th ACM Int. Conf. on Information and Knowledge Management*, pages 99–106, 2005. ISBN 1-59593-140-6. DOI: 10.1145/1099554.1099575 78, 79, 80

B. Carminati, E. Ferrari, and B. Thuraisingham. Access Control for Web Data: Models and Policy Languages. *Annales des Télécommunications*, 61(3-4):245–266, 2006. 2

B. Carminati, E. Ferrari, R. Heatherly, M. Kantarcioglu, and B. Thuraisingham. A Semantic Web based Framework for Social Network Access Control. In *Proc. 14th ACM Symposium on Access Control Models and Technologies*, pages 177–186, 2009a. ISBN 978-1-60558-537-6. DOI: 10.1145/1542207.1542237 85

B. Carminati, E. Ferrari, and A. Perego. Enforcing Access Control in Web-based Social Networks. *ACM Trans. Information & Syst. Sec.*, 13(1):1–38, 2009b. ISSN 1094-9224. DOI: 10.1145/1609956.1609962 84

B. Carminati, E. Ferrari, K.L. Tan, and J. Cao. A Framework to Enforce Access Control over Data Streams. *ACM Trans. Information & Syst. Sec.*, 2010. to appear. DOI: 10.1145/1266840.1266845 81, 82

S. Castano, M.G. Fugini, G. Martella, and P. Samarati. *Database Security*. Addison-Wesley & ACM Press, 1995. ISBN 0-201-59375-0. 1

S. Chen, D. Wijesekera, and S. Jajodia. Flexflow: A Flexible Flow Control Policy Specification Framework. In *Proc. IFIP WG 11.3 Working Conference on Data and Application Security*, pages 358–371, 2003. 60

J. Crampton. Understanding and Developing Role-based Administrative Models. In *Proc. 12th ACM Conf. on Computer and Communication Security*, pages 158–167. ACM, 2005. ISBN 1-59593-226-7. DOI: 10.1145/1102120.1102143 73

J. Crampton. Applying Hierarchical and Role-based Access Control to XML Documents. In *Proc. ACM Workshop on Secure Web Services*, pages 37–46, 2004. DOI: 10.1145/1111348.1111353 45

J. Crampton and G. Loizou. Administrative Scope: a Foundation for Role-based Administrative Models. *ACM Trans. Information & Syst. Sec.*, 6(2):201–231, 2003. ISSN 1094-9224. DOI: 10.1145/762476.762478 72, 73

E. Damiani, S. De Capitani di Vimercati, S. Paraboschi, and P. Samarati. A Fine-grained Access Control System for XML Documents. *ACM Trans. Information & Syst. Sec.*, 5(2):169–202, 2002. ISSN 1094-9224. DOI: 10.1145/505586.505590 42, 43

M.L. Damiani, E. Bertino, B. Catania, and P. Perlasca. GEO-RBAC: A Spatially aware RBAC. *ACM Trans. Information & Syst. Sec.*, 10(1):1–42, 2007. DOI: 10.1145/1063979.1063985 74

S. De Capitani di Vimercati, S. Jajodia, S. Paraboschi, and P. Samarati. Trust Management Services in Relational Databases. In *Proc. ACM Symposium on Information, Computer and Communications Security*, pages 149–160, 2007. ISBN 1-59593-574-6. DOI: 10.1145/1229285.1229308 26

M. Decker. Requirements for a Location-based Access Control Model. In *Proc. 6th International Conference on Advances in Mobile Computing and Multimedia*, pages 346–349, 2008. ISBN 978-1-60558-269-6. DOI: 10.1145/1497185.1497259 2, 86

D.E. Denning, T.F. Lunt, R.R. Schell, M Heckman, and W.R. Shockley. A Multilevel Relational Data Model. In *Proc. 8th IEEE Symposium on Security & Privacy*, pages 220–234, 1987. DOI: 10.1109/SP.1987.10023 56

N. Li E. Bertino, J.W. Byun. Privacy-preserving Database Systems. In *Foundations of Security Analysis and Design III*, Lecture Notes in Computer Science, pages 178–206, 2005. DOI: 10.1007/11554578_6 2

N. Elahi, M.M. Chowdhury, and J. Noll. Semantic Access Control in Web Based Communities. In *Proc. 3rd Int. Multi-Conference on Computing in the Global Information Technology*, pages 131–136, 2008. ISBN 978-0-7695-3275-2. DOI: 10.1109/ICCGI.2008.46 85

A. Ene, W. Horne, N. Milosavljevic, P. Rao, R. Schreiber, and R.E. Tarjan. Fast Exact and Heuristic Methods for Role Minimization Problems. In *Proc. 13th ACM Symposium on Access Control Models and Technologies*, pages 1–10. ACM, 2008. ISBN 978-1-60558-129-3. DOI: 10.1145/1377836.1377838 73

R. Fagin. On an Authorization Mechanism. *ACM Trans. Database Syst.*, 3(6):310–319, November 1976. DOI: 10.1145/320263.320288 1, 13

W. Fan, C.Y. Chan, and M. Garofalakis. Secure XML Querying with Security Views. In *Proc. ACM SIGMOD Int. Conf. on Management of Data*, pages 587–598, 2004. ISBN 1-58113-859-8. DOI: 10.1145/1007568.1007634 46

C. Farkas and S. Jajodia. The Inference Problem: a Survey. *SIGKDD Exploration Newsletter*, 4(2): 6–11, 2002. ISSN 1931-0145. DOI: 10.1145/772862.772864 59

D. Ferraiolo, R. Kuhn, and R. Sandhu. RBAC Standard Rationale: Comments on "A Critique of the ANSI Standard on Role-based Access Control". *IEEE Security & Privacy*, 5:51–53, 2007. ISSN 1540-7993. DOI: 10.1109/MSP.2007.173 66

D.F. Ferraiolo, J.F. Barkley, and D.R. Kuhn. A Role-based Access Control Model and Reference Implementation within a Corporate Intranet. *ACM Trans. Information & Syst. Sec.*, 2(1):34–64, 1999. ISSN 1094-9224. DOI: 10.1145/300830.300834 65

D.F. Ferraiolo, R.S. Sandhu, S.I. Gavrila, D.R. Kuhn, and R. Chandramouli. Proposed NIST Standard for Role-based Access Control. *ACM Trans. Information & Syst. Sec.*, 4(3):224–274, 2001. DOI: 10.1145/501978.501980 61, 62

E. Ferrari. Access Control. In L. Liu and M.T. Özsu, editors, *Encyclopedia of Database Systems*, Springer, pages 7–11. 2009a. DOI: 10.1007/978-0-387-39940-9 xiii, 1

E. Ferrari. Database as a Service: Challenges and Solutions for Privacy and Security. In *Proceedings of the First APSCC Workshop on Secure Service Computing*, Singapore, 2009b. 2, 77, 78

E. Ferrari. Database Security. In L. Liu and M.T. Özsu, editors, *Encyclopedia of Database Systems*, Springer, pages 728–732. 2009c. DOI: 10.1007/978-0-387-39940-9 xiii

E. Ferrari. Access Control Administration Policies. In L. Liu and M.T. Özsu, editors, *Encyclopedia of Database Systems*, Springer, pages 12–14. 2009d. DOI: 10.1007/978-0-387-39940-9 9

E. Ferrari and B. Thuraisingham. Secure Database Systems. In O. Diaz and M. Piattini, editors, *Advanced Databases: Technology and Design*. Artech House, 2000. 1, 8, 10, 27

E. Ferrari and B Thuraisingham. Security and Privacy for Web Databases and Services. In *Advances in Database Technology, Proc. 9th Int. Conf. on Extending Database Technology*, volume 2992 of *Lecture Notes in Computer Science*, pages 17–28, 2004. 2

P.W.L. Fong, M. M. Anwar, and Z. Zhao. A Privacy Preservation Model for Facebook-style Social Network Systems. In *Proc. 14th European Symposium on Research in Computer Security*, volume 5789 of *Lecture Notes in Computer Science*, pages 303–320, 2009. DOI: 10.1007/978-3-642-04444-1_19 84

ANSI. American National Standard for Information Technology. Role based Access Control. Technical report, ANSI INCITS 359-2004, February 2004. 62

A. Gabillon and E. Bruno. Regulating Access to XML documents. In *Proc. 15th Annual Working Conf. on Database and Application Security*, pages 299–314, 2002. ISBN 1-4020-7041-1. 42, 43

H. Garcia-Molina, J.D. Ullman, and J. Widom. *Database Systems: the Complete Book*. Prentice Hall, Upper Saddle River, NJ, USA, 2008. ISBN 9780131873254. 3

F. Giannotti and D. Pedreschi, editors. Mobility, Data Mining, and Privacy: Geographic Knowledge Discovery. Springer, 2008. ISBN 978-3-540-75176-2. 86

L. Golab and M.T. Özsu. Issues in Data Stream Management. *SIGMOD Record*, 32(2):5–14, 2003. DOI: 10.1145/776985.776986 80

G. Graham and P.J. Denning. Protection: Principles and Practice. In *Proc. AFIPS Spring Joint Computer Conf.*, pages 417–429, 1972. DOI: 10.1145/1478873.1478928 11

P.P. Griffiths and B.W. Wade. An Authorization Mechanism for a Relational Database System. *ACM Trans. Database Syst.*, 1(3):242–255, September 1976. DOI: 10.1145/320473.320482 1, 11, 13

H. Hacigümüs, B. Iyer, C. Li, and S. Mehrotra. Executing SQL over Encrypted Data in the Database-service-provider Model. In *Proc. ACM SIGMOD Int. Conf. on Management of Data*, pages 216–227, 2002. ISBN 1-58113-497-5. DOI: 10.1145/564691.564717 79, 80

H. Hacigümüs, B.R. Iyer, and S. Mehrotra. Efficient Execution of Aggregation Queries over Encrypted Relational Databases. In *Proc. 9th Int. Conf. on Database Systems for Advanced Applications*, volume 2973 of *Lecture Notes in Computer Science*, pages 125–136, 2004. DOI: 10.1007/b95600 79

H. Hacigümüs, B.R. Iyer, and S. Mehrotra. Query Optimization in Encrypted Database Systems. In *Proc. 10th Int. Conf. on Database Systems for Advanced Applications*, volume 3453 of *Lecture Notes in Computer Science*, pages 43–55, 2005. DOI: 10.1007/11408079_7 79

M.A. Harrison, W.L. Ruzzo, and J.D. Ullman. On Protection in Operating Systems. In *Proc. 5th ACM Symp. on Operating System Principles*, pages 14–24, 1975. DOI: 10.1145/360303.360333 11

B. Hayes. Cloud Computing. *Commun. ACM*, 51(7):9–11, 2008. ISSN 0001-0782. DOI: 10.1145/1364782.1364786 77

I. Horrocks, P.F. Patel-Schneider, H. Boley, S. Tabet, B. Grosof, and M. Dean. SWRL: A Semantic Web Rule Language Combining OWL and RuleML. W3C Member Submission, World Wide Web Consortium, 2004. URL http://www.w3.org/Submission/SWRL. 85

ISO. Database Languages - SQL, 2003. 13, 23, 25, 67

S. Jajodia and B. Kogan. Integrating an Object-oriented Data Model with Multilevel Security. In *Proc. 11th IEEE Symposium on Security & Privacy*, pages 76–85, 1990. DOI: 10.1109/RISP.1990.63840 57, 60

S. Jajodia, P. Samarati, M.L. Sapino, and V.S. Subrahmanian. Flexible Support for Multiple Access Control Policies. *ACM Trans. Database Syst.*, 26(2):214–260, 2001. ISSN 0362-5915. DOI: 10.1145/383891.383894 7, 29

A. Jøsang, R. Ismail, and C. Boyd. A Survey of Trust and Reputation Systems for Online Service Provision. *Decision Support Systems*, 43(2):618–644, 2007. DOI: 10.1016/j.dss.2005.05.019 82

J. Joshi, E. Bertino, U. Latif, and A. Ghafoor. A Generalized Temporal Role-based Access Control Model. *IEEE Trans. Knowl. and Data Eng.*, 17(1):4–23, 2005. DOI: 10.1109/TKDE.2005.1 8, 65, 74

Y. Kanza, A.O. Mendelzon, R.J. Miller, and Z. Zhang. Authorization-transparent Access Control for XML Under the Non-Truman Model. In *Advances in Database Technology, Proc. 10th Int. Conf. on Extending Database Technology*, pages 222–239, 2006. DOI: 10.1007/11687238_16 42, 46

P.A. Karger. Limiting the Damage Potential of Discretionary Trojan Horses. In *Proc. 8th IEEE Symposium on Security & Privacy*, pages 32–37, 1987. DOI: 110.1109/SP.1987.10011 59

T.F. Keefe, W.T. Tsai, and B. Thuraisingham. SODA: a Secure Object-oriented Database System. *Computers and Security*, 8(6):517–533, 1989. ISSN 0167-4048. DOI: 10.1016/0167-4048(89)90081-3 56, 57

A. Kern, A. Schaad, and J. Moffett. An Administration Concept for the Enterprise Role-based Access Control Model. In *Proc. 8th ACM Symposium on Access Control Models and Technologies*, pages 3–11, 2003. ISBN 1-58113-681-1. DOI: 10.1145/775412.775414 73

S.R. Kruk, S. Grzonkowski, A. Gzella, T. Woroniecki, and H-C. Choi. D-FOAF: Distributed Identity Management with Access Rights Delegation. In *Proc. 1st Asian Semantic Web Conference*, pages 140–154, 2006. DOI: 10.1007/11836025_15 84

M. Kudo and S. Hada. XML Document Security based on Provisional Authorization. In *Proc. 7th ACM Conf. on Computer and Communication Security*, pages 87–96, 2000. ISBN 1-58113-203-4. DOI: 10.1145/352600.352613 42, 43

B.W. Lampson. Protection. In *Proc. 5th Princeton Symposium on Information Sciences and Systems*, pages 437–443, 1971. Reprinted in Operating Systems Review, 8(1):18–24, January 1974. DOI: 10.1145/775265.775268 1, 11

N. Li and Z. Mao. Administration in Role-based Access Control. In *Proc. ACM Symposium on Information, Computer and Communications Security*, pages 127–138, 2007. ISBN 1-59593-574-6. DOI: 10.1145/1229285.1229305 73

N. Li, J.W. Byun, and E. Bertino. A Critique of the ANSI Standard on Role-based Access Control. *IEEE Security & Privacy*, 5(6):41–49, 2007. ISSN 1540-7993. DOI: 10.1109/MSP.2007.158 66

W. Lindner and J. Meier. Securing the Borealis Data Stream Engine. In *Proc. Int. Conf. on Database Eng. and Applications*, pages 137–147, 2006. ISBN 0-7695-2577-6. DOI: 110.1109/IDEAS.2006.40 81

H. Lu, J. Vaidya, and V. Atluri. Optimal Boolean Matrix Decomposition: Application to Role Engineering. In *Proc. 24th Int. Conf. on Data Engineering*, pages 297–306, 2008. ISBN 978-1-4244-1836-7. DOI: 10.1109/ICDE.2008.4497438 73

T.F. Lunt, D.E. Denning, R.R. Schell, M. Heckman, and W.R. Shockley. The SeaView Security Model. *IEEE Trans. Softw. Eng.*, 16(6):593–607, 1990. 27, 54

B. Luo, D. Lee, W.C. Lee, and P. Liu. QFilter: Fine-grained Run-time XML Access Control via NFA-based Query Rewriting. In *Proc. 13th ACM Int. Conf. on Information and Knowledge Management*, pages 543–552. ACM, 2004. ISBN 1-58113-874-1. DOI: 10.1145/1031171.1031273 46

W. Luo, Q. Xie, and U. Hengartner. FaceCloak: An Architecture for User Privacy on Social Networking Sites. In *Proc. 12th IEEE Int. Conference on Computational Science and Engineering*, pages 26–33, 2009. DOI: 10.1109/CSE.2009.387 87

A.P. McAfee. Enterprise 2.0: The Dawn of Emergent Collaboration. *MITSloan Management Review*, 47(3):21–28, 2006. URL http://sloanreview.mit.edu/the-magazine/articles/2006/spring/47306/enterprise-the-dawn-of-emergent-collaboration/. 82

C.D. McCollum, J.R. Messing, and L. Notargiacomo. Beyond the Pale of MAC and DAC – Defining New Forms of Access Control. In *Proc. 11th IEEE Symposium on Security & Privacy*, pages 190–200, 1990. DOI: 10.1109/RISP.1990.63850 59

P. McDaniel. On Context in Authorization Policy. In *Proc. 8th ACM Symposium on Access Control Models and Technologies*, pages 80–89, 2003. ISBN 1-58113-681-1. DOI: 10.1145/775412.775422 9

J. McLean. The Specification and Modeling of Computer Security. *Computer*, 23(1):9–16, January 1990. DOI: 10.1109/2.48795 53

G. Mella, E. Ferrari, E. Bertino, and Y. Koglin. Controlled and Cooperative Updates of XML Documents in Byzantine and Failure-prone Distributed Systems. *ACM Trans. Information & Syst. Sec.*, 9(4):421–460, 2006. ISSN 1094-9224. DOI: 10.1145/1187441.1187443 45

J. Melton and S. Buxton. *Querying XML: XQuery, XPath, and SQL/XML in Context.* Morgan Kaufmann, 2006. 43

G. Miklau and D. Suciu. Controlling Access to Published Data using Cryptography. In *Proc. 29th Int. Conf. on Very Large Data Bases*, pages 898–909, 2003. ISBN 0-12-722442-4. 79, 80

I. Molloy, H. Chen, T. Li, Q. Wang, N. Li, E. Bertino, S. Calo, and J. Lobo. Mining Roles with Semantic Meanings. In *Proc. 13th ACM Symposium on Access Control Models and Technologies*, pages 21–30, 2008. ISBN 978-1-60558-129-3. DOI: 10.1145/1377836.1377840 73

I. Molloy, N. Li, T. Li, Z. Mao, Q. Wang, and J. Lobo. Evaluating Role Mining Algorithms. In *Proc. 14th ACM Symposium on Access Control Models and Technologies*, pages 95–104, 2009. ISBN 978-1-60558-537-6. DOI: 10.1145/1542207.1542224 74

T. Moses. *eXtensible Access Control Markup Language TC v2.0 (XACML).* OASIS, February 2005. URL http://docs.oasis-open.org/xacml/2.0/access_control-xacml-2.0-core-spec-os.pdf. 39

M. Murata, A. Tozawa, M. Kudo, and S. Hada. XML Access Control using Static Analysis. *ACM Trans. Information & Syst. Sec.*, 9(3):292–324, 2006. ISSN 1094-9224. DOI: 10.1145/1178618.1178621 42, 45, 47

R.V. Nehme, H.S. Lim, E. Bertino, and E.A. Rundensteiner. StreamShield: a Stream-centric Approach towards Security and Privacy in Data Stream Environments. In *Proc. ACM SIGMOD Int. Conf. on Management of Data*, pages 1027–1030, 2009. ISBN 978-1-60558-551-2. DOI: 10.1145/1559845.1559972 82

Q. Ni, A. Trombetta, E. Bertino, and J. Lobo. Privacy-aware Role-based Access Control. In *Proc. 12th ACM Symposium on Access Control Models and Technologies*, pages 41–50, 2007. ISBN 978-1-59593-745-2. DOI: 10.1145/1266840.1266848 75

Q. Ni, E. Bertino, J. Lobo, and S.B. Calo. Privacy-aware Role-based Access Control. *IEEE Security & Privacy*, 7(4):35–43, 2009. DOI: 10.1109/MSP.2009.102 2

J. Nin, B. Carminati, E. Ferrari, and V. Torra. Computing Reputation for Collaborative Private Networks. In *Proc. 9th Int. Computer Software Applications Conf.*, pages 246–253, 2009. DOI: 10.1109/COMPSAC.2009.40 85

U.S. Deptartment of Defense. Trusted Computer System Evaluation Criteria (Orange Book), 1975. 58

S. Oh and R. Sandhu. A Model for Role Administration using Organization Structure. In *Proc. 7th ACM Symposium on Access Control Models and Technologies*, pages 155–162, 2002. ISBN 1-58113-496-7. DOI: 10.1145/507711.507737 71

M.S. Olivier and S.H. von Solms. A Taxonomy for Secure Object-oriented Databases. *ACM Trans. Database Syst.*, 19(1):3–46, 1994. ISSN 0362-5915. DOI: 10.1145/174638.174640 56

Committee on Multilevel Data Management Security Air Force Studies Board. Multilevel Data Management Security, Commission on Engineering and Technical Systems, National Research Council. Technical report, National Academy Press, 1983. 1

Oracle Corporation. *Oracle Database: Security Guide.* 2009. 30, 32, 54, 56

S. Osborn, R. Sandhu, and Q. Munawer. Configuring Role-based Access Control to Enforce Mandatory and Discretionary Access Control Policies. *ACM Trans. Information & Syst. Sec.*, 3 (2):85–106, 2000. DOI: 10.1145/354876.354878 61

P.F. Patel-Schneider, P. Hayes, and I. Horrocks. OWL Web Ontology Language - Semantics and Abstract Syntax. W3C Recommentation, W3C, February 2004. URL http://www.w3.org/TR/2004/REC-owl-semantics-20040210/. 85

N. Qi and M. Kudo. XML Access Control with Policy Matching Tree. In *Proc. 10th European Symposium on Research in Computer Security*, 2005. DOI: 10.1007/11555827_2 47

F. Rabitti, E. Bertino, W. Kim, and D. Woelk. A Model of Authorization for Next-generation Database Systems. *ACM Trans. Database Syst.*, 16(1):88–131, 1991. ISSN 0362-5915. DOI: 10.1145/103140.103144 37

I. Ray and M. Toahchoodee. A Spatio-temporal Access Control Model Supporting Delegation for Pervasive Computing Applications. In *Proc. 5th international Conference on Trust, Privacy and Security in Digital Business*, pages 48–58, 2008. ISBN 978-3-540-85734-1. DOI: 10.1007/978-3-540-85735-8_6 75

S. Rizvi, A. Mendelzon, S. Sudarshan, and P. Roy. Extending Query Rewriting Techniques for Fine-grained Access Control. In *Proc. ACM SIGMOD Int. Conf. on Management of Data*, pages 551–562, 2004. ISBN 1-58113-859-8. DOI: 10.1145/1007568.1007631 35

P. Samarati, E. Bertino, A. Ciampichetti, and S. Jajodia. Information Flow Control in Object-oriented Systems. *IEEE Trans. Knowl. and Data Eng.*, 9:524–538, 1997. ISSN 1041-4347. DOI: 10.1109/69.617048 59

R. Sandhu and F. Chen. The Multilevel Relational (MLR) Data Model. *ACM Trans. Information & Syst. Sec.*, 1(1):93–132, 1998. ISSN 1094-9224. DOI: 10.1145/290163.290171 56

R. Sandhu and Q. Munawer. The ARBAC99 Model for Administration of Roles. In *Proc. Annual Computer Security Applications Conference*, page 229. IEEE Computer Society, 1999. ISBN 0-7695-0346-2. 71

R. Sandhu, V. Bhamidipati, and Q. Munawer. The ARBAC97 Model for Role-based Administration of Roles. *ACM Trans. Information & Syst. Sec.*, 2(1):105–135, 1999. ISSN 1094-9224. DOI: 10.1145/300830.300839 70, 71

R.S. Sandhu. Lattice-Based Access Control Models. *Computer*, 26(11):9–19, 1993. ISSN 0018-9162. DOI: 10.1109/2.241422 51

R.S. Sandhu, E.J. Coyne, H.L. Feinstein, and C.E. Youman. Role-based Access Control Models. *IEEE Computer*, 29(2):38–47, 1996. 2, 10, 26, 61

O.S. Saydjari. Multilevel Security: Reprise. *IEEE Security & Privacy*, 2(5):64–67, 2004. ISSN 1540-7993. DOI: 10.1109/MSP.2004.78 56

A. Schaad, J. Moffett, and J. Jacob. The Role-based Access Control System of a European Bank: a Case Study and Discussion. In *Proc. 6th ACM Symposium on Access Control Models and Technologies*, pages 3–9, 2001. ISBN 1-58113-350-2. DOI: 10.1145/373256.373257 70

J. Schlegelmilch and U. Steffens. Role Mining with ORCA. In *Proc. 10th ACM Symposium on Access Control Models and Technologies*, pages 168–176, 2005. ISBN 1-59593-045-0. DOI: 10.1145/1063979.1064008 73

B. Shafiq, J. Joshi, E. Bertino, and A. Ghafoor. Secure Interoperation in a Multidomain Environment Employing RBAC Policies. *IEEE Trans. Knowl. and Data Eng.*, 17(11):1557–1577, 2005. ISSN 1041-4347. DOI: 10.1109/TKDE.2005.185 75

D.X. Song, D. Wagner, and A. Perrig. Practical Techniques for Searches on Encrypted Data. In *Proc. 21th IEEE Symposium on Security & Privacy*, page 44, 2000. ISBN 0-7695-0665-8. DOI: 10.1109/SECPRI.2000.848445 79, 80

A.C. Squicciarini, I. Paloscia, and E. Bertino. Protecting Databases from Query Flood Attacks. In *Proc. 24th Int. Conf. on Data Engineering*, pages 1358–1360, 2008. DOI: 10.1109/ICDE.2008.4497555 3

P.D. Stachour and B. Thuraisingham. Design of LDV: a Multilevel Secure Relational Database Management. *IEEE Trans. Knowl. and Data Eng.*, 2(2):190–209, 1990. ISSN 1041-4347. DOI: 10.1109/69.54719 56

W. Stallings. *Cryptography and Network Security*. Prentice Hall, 2003. 3

B. Thuraisingham. Recursion Theoretic Properties of the Inference Problem in Database Security. *IEEE Computer Society Technical Committee Newsletter on Security & Privacy*, pages 31–34, 1991. 59

B. Thuraisingham. Mandatory Security in Object-oriented Database Systems. In *Proc. 1989 Conf. on Object-Oriented Programming Systems, Languages, and Applications*, pages 203–210. ACM, 1989. ISBN 0-89791-333-7. DOI: 10.1145/74877.74899 57

A. Tootoonchian, S. Saroiu, Y. Ganjali, and A. Wolman. Lockr: Better Privacy for Social Networks. In *Proc. 5th Int. Conf. on Emerging Networking Experiments and Technologies*, pages 169–180, 2009. ISBN 978-1-60558-636-6. DOI: 10.1145/1658939.1658959 84

J. Vaidya, V. Atluri, and Q. Guo. The Role Mining Problem: Finding a Minimal Descriptive Set of Roles. In *Proc. 12th ACM Symposium on Access Control Models and Technologies*, pages 175–184, 2007. ISBN 978-1-59593-745-2. DOI: 10.1145/1266840.1266870 73

J. Vaidya, V. Atluri, Q. Guo, and N. Adam. Migrating to Optimal RBAC with Minimal Perturbation. In *Proc. 13th ACM Symposium on Access Control Models and Technologies*, pages 11–20, 2008. ISBN 978-1-60558-129-3. DOI: 10.1145/1377836.1377839 73

W. Villegas, B. Ali, and M. Maheswaran. An Access Control Scheme for Protecting Personal Data. In *Proc. 6th Annual Conference on Privacy, Security and Trust*, pages 24–35, 2008. ISBN 978-0-7695-3390-2. DOI: 10.1109/PST.2008.14 83

H. Wang and L.V. Lakshmanan. Efficient Secure Query Evaluation over Encrypted XML Databases. In *Proc. 32nd Int. Conf. on Very Large Data Bases*, pages 127–138, 2006. 79

D.J. Weitzner, H. Abelson, T. Berners-Lee, J. Feigenbaum, J.A. Hendler, and G.J. Sussman. Information Accountability. *Commun. ACM*, 51(6):82–87, 2008. DOI: 10.1145/1349026.1349043 88

P.F. Wilms and B.G. Lindsay. A Database Authorization Mechanism Supporting Individual and Group Authorization. In *Proc. 2nd International Seminar on Distributed Data Sharing Systems*, pages 273–292, 1981. 26

C. Yeung, I. Liccardi, K. Lu, O. Seneviratne, and T. Berners-Lee. Decentralization: the Future of Online Social Networking. In *W3C Workshop on the Future of Social Networking*, 2009. URL http://www.w3.org/2008/09/msnws/papers/decentralization.pdf. 83

T. Yu, D. Srivastava, L.V. Lakshmanan, and H.V. Jagadish. A Compressed Accessibility Map for XML. *ACM Trans. Database Syst.*, 29(2):363–402, 2004. ISSN 0362-5915. DOI: 10.1145/1005566.1005570 47

Y. Zhang and J. Joshi. Role Based Access Control. In L. Liu and M.T. Özsu, editors, *Encyclopedia of Database Systems*, Springer, pages 2447–2452. 2009. DOI: 10.1007/978-0-387-39940-9 61

Author's Biography

ELENA FERRARI

Elena Ferrari is a full professor of Computer Science at the University of Insubria, Italy, where she heads the Database & Web Security Group. She received an MS degree in Computer Science from the University of Milano (Italy) in 1992. In 1998, she received a Ph.D. in Computer Science from the same university. Her research activities are related to various aspects of data and application security and privacy, including Web security and privacy, trust negotiations and trust management, access control and privacy for innovative applications (social networks, workflow management systems, multimedia databases, data streams, XML data sources), and the Semantic Web. On these topics she has published more than 140 scientific publications in international journals and conference proceedings.

Because of her research activity, she received the IEEE Computer Society prestigious 2009 Technical Achievement Award for "outstanding and innovative contributions to secure data management".

Dr. Ferrari served as Program Chair of the 4th ACM Symposium on Access Control Models and Technologies (SACMAT'04), Software Demonstration Chair of the 9th International Conference on Extending Database Technology (EDBT'04), Co-Chair of the third IFIP WG 11.11 International Conference on Trust Management, the first and second ACM International Workshop on Privacy, Security, and Trust in KDD, and the first COMPSAC' Workshop on Web Security and Semantic Web. She has also served as Program Committee member of several international conferences and workshops, including SIGMOD, ICDE, VLDB, and ICWS. Prof. Ferrari is in the Editorial Board of the IEEE Transactions on Knowledge and Data Engineering, the Transactions on Data Privacy, and the International Journal of Information Technology (IJIT). She is a member of ACM and senior member of IEEE.

Printed in the United States
by Baker & Taylor Publisher Services